# The Art of
# UnConscious Success

Beyond Survival, Reinvent Your Mind and Enhance Your Life

## Art C. Guerrero
Award Winning Author

**10-10-10**
Publishing

The Art of Unconscious Success
Beyond Survival, Reinvent Your Mind and Enhance Your Life
ucsuccess.com

Copyright © 2019 by Art C. Guerrero

ISBN: 978-1-77277-283-8

All rights reserved. No part of this publication may be reproduced, mechanically, electronically, photocopying or by any other means, without permission of the publisher or author except in the case of brief quotations embodied in critical articles are reviews. It is illegal to copy this book, post it to a website, or distribute it by any other means without permission from the publisher or author.

Limits of Liability and Disclaimer of Warranty
The author and publisher shall not be liable for your misuse of the enclosed material. This book is strictly for informational and educational purposes only.

Warning – Disclaimer
The purpose of this book is to educate and entertain. The author and/or publisher do not guarantee that anyone following these techniques, suggestions, tips, ideas or strategies will become successful. The author and/or publisher shall have neither liability nor responsibility to anyone with respect to any loss or damage caused, or alleged to be caused, directly or indirectly by the information contained in this book.

Medical Disclaimer
The medical or health information in this book is provided as an information resource only, and is not to be used or relied on for any diagnostic or treatment purposes. This information is not intended to be patient education, does not create any patient-physician relationship, and should not be used as a substitute for professional diagnosis and treatment.

Published by:
10-10-10 Publishing
Markham, Ontario   Canada

Second Edition - June 2019
Printed in Canada and the United States of America

# Table of Contents

| | |
|---|---|
| Dedication | vii |
| Foreword by Les Brown | ix |
| About the Author | xiii |

**Chapter 1: The Awakening** — 1
- The CYCLE — 1
- The Calling — 4
- Beyond Survival — 7
- Be Present NOW — 9

**Chapter 2: The Art of Letting Go** — 13
- Unconscious Success — 13
- Stuck? Stop Holding On — 15
- Give to Live — 18
- Lose Control — 21
- Surrender — 23
- Trust — 25

**Chapter 3: The Unknown & Its Wonders** — 29
- Comfort Zones — 29
- The Power of Questions — 32
- Un-Learn & Re-Learn — 34
- Blank Canvas — 37
- Embrace NEWness — 40
- Do Something Different — 43

## Chapter 4: The Power of Choice — 47
- Everything is Choice — 47
- Anything is Possible — 50
- Become Someone Else — 52
- How to Decide — 56
- The Power of Intention — 59
- Take Action — 60

## Chapter 5: Perception of Reality — 63
- Mentality = Reality — 63
- The Mirror Effect — 65
- The Illusion of Time — 68
- Orchestrate Importance — 70
- The Illusion of Fear — 72
- Observation & Awareness — 74

## Chapter 6: Exchanging Ideas — 77
- Sell to Propel — 77
- The People Business — 79
- The Power of Agreements — 82
- 100% Attitude – Smile — 84
- The Power of NO! — 88
- Persistence — 90

## Chapter 7: Reinvent Your Mind — 93
- Discover Your Path — 93
- The Transformation — 96
- Creativity with Passion — 97
- Introspection — 99
- Absorb Knowledge, Evolve & Succeed — 102
- Just Be — 104

**Chapter 8: The Dance of the Heart & Mind**    **107**
- Balance    107
- Thoughts and Feelings    110
- Music & Atmosphere    112
- Communication    114
- Health & Wellness    116
- Energetic Momentum    120

**Chapter 9: Realize & Utilize**    **123**
- Stay in Your Lane    123
- In Your Favor    125
- Revisit Your Story    128
- Resources    131
- The Power of Words    133
- Talents & Gifts    136

**Chapter 10: Enhance Your Life**    **139**
- P.U.S.H.    139
- The Power of Connection    141
- Desire to Inspire    144
- Attitude of Gratitude    146
- Being of Service    149
- Have Fun and Celebrate    151

**Special Thanks To**    **155**

This book is dedicated to
my beautiful, amazing wife, Mireya,
who has always believed in me unconditionally.
You are my shining star and my rock.
To my amazing children, Gia, Felix and Richard,
who inspired this book to be a
reference guide for their life's journey.

# Foreword

Dear Reader,

Are you ready to get out of the cycle that keeps you going in circles and move towards your goals and dreams you have been so eagerly trying to achieve? Then this book is for you.

"In order to do something you've never done, you've got to become someone you've never been. I think that all of us have great potential within us, but greatness is a choice; it's not our destiny. And in the pursuit of our dreams we are introduced to trials, failures and disappointments, which take us to the door of discovery and greatness."

I am honored and privileged to introduce Art Guerrero, a fellow speaker and author, who will show you how to discover the hidden blocks in your unconscious mind, so you may breakthrough, overcome and navigate through life with more energy and enthusiasm to obtain the success you want.

I see passion and hunger in the way that Art Guerrero teaches, and shares his knowledge that he has gained through his challenges. With an open heart he shares his story and the hard lessons he has learned.

*Art C. Guerrero*

This book is designed to empower you with the unconscious process of success used by the rich and famous. Art Guerrero will show you strategies to transform your life and experience health, wealth and happiness that you so rightfully deserve.

Learning ways to change and grow from a deeper level, looking deep within yourself to find the root of not only what holds you back, but also you will be able to peel away all the layers to find your true self and your purpose.

Art is the only trainer that delivers you the powerful **BEYOND**™ technique.

**B – Breakthrough** - Where you will breakthrough your barriers towards your goals.

**E – Enhance** - You will enhance your energy and life.

**Y – You** - Focused on helping you find your true value and become the new you.

**O – Outstanding** - You will stand out in your business and have an outstanding life.

**N – New** - You will learn new strategies to navigate through life effortlessly.

**D – Design** - Dedicated to design an new blue print for your dream life.

*The Art of Unconscious Success*

Are you ready to go beyond your limits, beyond just surviving, to thriving!

In this book, "The Art of Unconscious Success", you will learn a new way to reinvent yourself and enhance your life.

You have something special, you have greatness inside you. That's my story and I'm sticking to it.

**Les Brown**
The Worlds #1 Motivator

## About the Author

Art C. Guerrero was born and raised in Midland, Texas, and lived in Dallas, Texas, for 12 years. He is married to the beautiful Mireya Guerrero, and has three amazing children, Gia, Felix and Richard. Art is the owner and president of West Texas Business Services, Inc. (WTBS Printing). He is also the founder and owner of Unconscious Success.

Art C. Guerrero has overcome his past challenges of drugs, poverty, and suicidal tendencies. Through his research of personal development, and guidance from his successful mentors, he has been able to transform his life and the lives of others.

Art is a serial entrepreneur, trainer, transformational speaker, and success coach. He inspires, empowers, and guides people to live authentically and with purpose, teaching individuals around the world how to reinvent their minds and live with passion from the heart.

Art C. Guerrero is available to deliver keynote presentations and motivational speeches. He is also available to appear on your podcast, radio, or television talk show. Art can also be hired as a success coach. For rates and availability, please contact the author directly at: art@ucsuccess.com

*Art C. Guerrero*

To order more books, please visit:
ucsuccess.com

Finally, if you have been inspired by this book, the best thing you can do is to pass it on.

You are amazing. Shine bright, for you and for others. Live with passion.

# Chapter 1

# The Awakening

**The CYCLE**

We have heard of the CYCLE of life, yet the CYCLE felt more like a hamster wheel: going and going, non-stop, living in a fast world, always on the go, waking up in a hurry to get dressed, rushing to work, working hard and fast, then rushing home, and Rush-Rush-Rush. Right?

And yet, not moving forward in life: same place, same job, same home, same car, same everything.

I started to feel as if something was missing. There had to be more than this.

The CYCLE that changed my course of life forever, was the motor-CYCLE.

On April 18th, 2009, I was riding on I-35 E Stemmons Freeway, in Dallas, Texas, going 90 mph, weaving through traffic, and feeling lost and frustrated with where I was in life—not to mention 5 shots of whiskey and no helmet. Suddenly, a gap I was about to shoot through began to close, and of course, my judgement was off. I hit the brake, and my motorcycle began to fishtail as I slid. Still sliding past traffic, since the speed limit was 65 mph, I kept holding on to the brake, and the motorcycle flipped me off. As I was falling backwards through the air, all I could think of was "Oh, shit!" ...as I crossed my arms and braced for impact. Landing on my shoulder, I rolled and then smacked my head on the pavement, which knocked me unconscious.

Moments later, I heard people calling me, trying to wake me up. I opened my eyes while lying in the middle of the freeway on my back, as someone was holding a sweater over my forehead, trying to stop the bleeding. Eight people surrounded me, and one of them asked, "Is there someone you would like us to call?" The first thing I said was, "Where is my iPhone?!" Some of them could not help but laugh a little. It's pretty funny, thinking about that remark now.

They told me to not get up. Who knows what might be broken, but I wasn't feeling any pain due to still being in shock—and ...oh yeah ...five shots of whiskey. They mentioned that my body was in convulsions moments before awakening. Waiting for an ambulance, I thought of a joke about a motorcycle and an ambulance, but I decided they might not find it too funny at the moment, so I kept it to myself.

When I arrived at Parkland Hospital, I looked in the mirror and noticed that a chunk of meat was missing from my head, and I could practically see my skull. The doctor explained that the skin torn on my forehead had only retracted, and she would attempt to stitch it back into place. Afterwards, the doctor asked, "You didn't think I was going to be able to stitch that up, right?" I replied, "No, I did not!" Then, what she said next surprised me: "I didn't either!" "Wow," I thought.

The hospital did some MRI scans on my head, neck, and spine to ensure there were no broken bones or fractures. Moments later, the report came back. "Mr. Guerrero, you have no broken bones or fractures; you are very lucky. Someone upstairs is looking out for you. You are free to go home." Wow, I arrived at the hospital about 7:00 PM, and I was leaving that same night, at 11:30 PM. Then, on my way to check out, I started feeling dizzy, and I felt like I was about to faint. The hospital decided: "We are going to keep you here for at least a day or two to monitor your recovery." That was a good thing, as my ankles started swelling, and I began to feel more pain.

The hospital ended up putting me in a room that I would share with another patient. This patient was moaning and groaning because he was in so much pain. I came to find out that he was also in a motorcycle accident. He had only been going 40 mph, and had dropped his motor-bike on his leg, breaking it in five places. Dang, I was going 90 mph, and I had no broken bones. Wow, things could have been worse for me. I began to pray for the other patient, and to be grateful that I was still alive.

The next morning, my parents arrived, and my dad said, "You are blessed son. God is looking out for you, because you have a greater purpose. You could have slid on your face or damaged your brain, damaging your mental abilities and capacities. You have been given another chance and opportunity to live life with purpose."

Those words really made me think. It was time to make a difference in my life. But how? As I thought about how to change, I thought about the way I lived my life and what needed to change, and I wanted to change. Yet the thing that really made me think was when my father had said *"...live life with purpose."* I began my search to find my purpose, feeling that the universe was giving me a wake-up call, and feeling as if I had been asleep, on auto pilot, and going through the motions. It was time to break the CYCLE.

## The Calling

Three weeks after the accident, my right pinky finger was still hurting, and I decided to have it x-rayed. Come to find out, it was broken. I was not invincible, and I felt it was God's way of letting me know I was still human. I was fortunate to survive the accident, and all things considered, with only breaking one finger, I was extremely grateful. After the motorcycle accident, and going through this crazy dramatic event in my life, it changed my perspective on life.

I began to question everything: different life styles, religions, and cultures. Why do we do the things we do? Why do we feel as if we have to act in a certain manner, in certain places. I began to feel and know that I had to evolve, and I wanted to learn more. While the MRIs showed everything to be okay physically, it was as if my mind had shifted and moved things into a new perspective and onto a new path. While my mind kept reminding me every morning of who I was, I began to repeat the patterns and routines as before. Breaking the cycle was not that easy. How would I get off this rollercoaster? I had been awakened, and it felt as though my spirit was trying to kick my body into gear, asking me, "Do you want another slap in the face!?"

What is my calling, my purpose? How do we search for our calling? Many of us look to the future and say, "What do I want to be when I grow up?" And some look into the past: "What have I done before, and what skills have I acquired?" Some people feel that those strategies will work, yet I have found that being present and asking, "What am I doing NOW, and what can I change NOW, that will affect my future." We don't get healthy by eating one healthy meal and exercising for one day—we have to do it on a consistent basis, every day.

Don't follow someone else's dream; live your own dream. What makes you happy, and what do you have a passion for? Your family wants you to be a certain thing; your friends want you to be something else; and society wants you to be "X" and to act accordingly. Yet you cannot please everyone. The one person you can please and make happy is yourself. Live YOUR life, and follow YOUR dreams.

Life will not go as planned; you will be derailed and get off track. A master trainer friend of mine told me: *"Success is not a straight line. It is squiggly and random, and it kind of looks like spaghetti."* Be open to what comes your way. When you put out the intention, the universe will respond; it will lead you and bring you the things and people that will assist you on your journey to success.

What is calling you? Be aware that there will be things that are calling you but are only shiny objects distracting you... from you.

You might have heard the saying: Know thy self. Get to know your inner self. Build a relationship with your heart, mind, and spirit, with care and love. Be aware of the amazing and powerful person within yourself. Live your life by the influence and inspiration of your inner self. When you don't, you tend to feel as if something is not right, because you are not living congruent with your thoughts and feelings.

What is it that you are passionate about? If money was not an issue, what would you love to do, regardless of any outside influence? What would be that vehicle that drives your mission and passion? Only you can decide if you are truly happy on the path that you have chosen, and you can always choose another path. There is a saying I love, and I have it on my wall at home, which reads, *"Do what you love, and love what you do."*

The way to change the world, starts with each individual changing on a personal level.

Some people believe that we are a product of our environment, yet I believe that our environment is a product of us. We attract the things that come into our lives; therefore, be aware of what energy or frequency you resonate at. When you are talking to the Universe and to God, the Universe and God are also communicating with you. Be open to the universe, because we are connected to everything; we are all energy. As I have come to observe and learn, the more we are open, the more opportunities will present themselves.

Remember that there is no right or wrong: what might be right for someone, may not be right for another. I once asked Robert

Raymond Riopel, a master trainer friend of mine, "What potential do you see in me?" And he replied, "The minute you are looking for someone else's approval or validation, is the minute you give up your power." Wow, I took that in and said, "Thank you," and walked away as I continued to digest and meditate on that.

The question is, "What do you see in yourself?" You decide if you are ready to continue to grow, evolve, and follow your dreams. Therefore, know yourself first, before going on your journey of success. When you discover who you are, then you will know if the opportunities are meant for you, or if they are shiny objects distracting you. As you discover and begin to reinvent yourself, ask, "What is my mission and my vision?" Know your purpose, and when something presents itself as an opportunity, ask yourself two questions: "Is it aligned with my mission, and is it aligned with my vision?"

## Beyond Survival

There are individuals that do just enough to get by, and just survive. How does this apply in other areas of your life? Where are you doing just enough to get by? Fellow students of life, in order to succeed, we must go past expectations, and go above and beyond the call of duty. Go the extra mile, and go for the WOW factor.

A twenty-nine-year-old millionaire and vice president of a sales company I once worked at, walked into one of my sales trainings, and I asked him, "Mr. Powers, is it not true that we must work smarter and not harder?" He chuckled and replied, "Well, the best thing to do is work smart *and* work hard." Well, there you have it. It's not whether you do this or that; it's whether you do everything that is in your power to learn and grow into your success.

Now, what can we do to go beyond our abilities and boundaries? A college professor once said, *"The only limits there are, are the ones I put in front of myself. The sky is NOT the limit."* Limitations are something that we make up. We create our perception based on how we decide to interpret the input from our five senses. Be aware of what you are telling yourself. Are you just surviving, from the beliefs that you took on from your parents or elders, who told you what they had to do in order to survive? While we appreciate what they did for us, I want to know: what would you do to thrive and live beyond survival? Sometimes we hear some people say, "Well, I'm here, aren't I?" And I ask, "Well ...for what purpose?" I don't want to just take up space. For me, it is about connecting with others and the world around me; to inspire others so we may live life to the fullest, together in unity. BEYOND SURVIVAL means to be more, and to ask more of yourself, not just for yourself but for others as well.

How can you help others if you cannot help yourself first? How can you love someone if you cannot love yourself first? It begins with you—ground zero. As you continue to move forward, and you continue to live beyond and to do more, you will gain momentum and begin growing and evolving. There is a big difference between when you are just surviving and when you are thriving.

*"To live is the rarest thing in the world. Most people just exist."*
— Oscar Wilde

Burt Munro, from New Zealand, once customized a 1920 Indian motorcycle, to help him set the land-speed world record at Utah's Bonneville Salt Flats, in 1967. Burt said something that really resonated with me: *"I live more in 5 minutes on this kind of bike than most people do in their entire lives."* I first thought, "Should I get another motorcycle?" Then, after meditating on that, I asked, "What is it that will make me feel more alive and enjoy life? What am I passionate about in life? What will I do as I continue to evolve?" I started looking at my inner self. "What will fulfill my spirit—my love tank—and make me feel whole?" For me, it was about connecting with people on a personal level. We sometimes want others to understand us, yet are we taking the time to understand them? When I connect and inspire others, they inspire me, which makes me feel alive and with purpose. After my motorcycle accident, I knew I did not want to just survive; I wanted to be able to thrive—not just to have a chance at life, but to dance with life.

**Be Present Now**

A quote I heard from Tony Robbins was: *"When would NOW be a good time?"* We must be present, yet what does that mean? There are some that live in the past, and you have heard them say before: "I should have…; I could have…; I would have…; if only "X" would have happened, I would have been "Z". They are always telling the same old glory stories, instead of creating new ones.

Then there are those that live in the future: When I get "X", and when I accomplish this and that, then I will be happy, and then I will be successful. Yet success is not a destination; success is a journey. We live as if we will be happy when we get there. Enjoy the journey, and be happy just to be happy. Many believe that you need a reason to be happy or to feel loved, yet we do not need a reason. Many brain studies show that just by feeling love and thinking happy, it creates the chemical response that makes our body and mind actually feel happiness and love. As we resonate on that frequency, we attract happiness and love into our lives.

What is happening NOW, and what can I do NOW? Now... take a deep breath ...and breathe ...that's right... breathe. As we breathe, it puts us back into the present moment—back into our body and back into the moment of NOW—being aware and conscious of what is happening around us. Many times, things happen, and we have to ask what happened and what someone said, because we were caught up in our own thoughts—what some people call day dreaming. Our minds are either in the past or in the future, but not in the present. There's a quote from the movie, *Kung Fu Panda*: *"Yesterday is history, tomorrow is a mystery, and today is a gift—that's why it's called the present."*

It's how you live this moment, NOW, that determines your future. Be aware of what is happening; have an expanded awareness. The Universe is feeding you information and clues, and it is showing you signs, yet are you paying attention? We must get off auto-pilot, and soar. Many people, by the time they are 35 years of age, have learned to respond unconsciously, running old programs in their minds, because they are running the same cycles, living the same lives, and acting on memorized responses. The study of neuro-linguistic programming says that our unconscious is constantly doing three main things: generalizing, distorting, or deleting information.

WOW! Take a deep breath and be present. NOW that you are aware that there is more going on within you, you can learn and go over how to reprogram your unconscious mind to enhance your life. In continuously being present, you will learn to be more calm and relaxed in handling life, being aware of what and why things are happening. This way, you can respond to life, instead of reacting to it, and you can make educated decisions.

Remembering to breathe is to become centered. When we take that deep breath, it relaxes us and allows the oxygen and energy to flow, which in turn releases stress. Because stress is stuck energy, we must release it and let it go. There are studies that show that 60% of cancer patients develop cancer because of stress. Stress impacts our immune systems, and our bodies cannot fight disease properly. There is a documentary, by National Geographic, called, *Stress: Portrait of a Killer*, which talks more on the effects of stress.

So, breathe, relax, be present, and be happy. The things that are happening in your life are just one of many perceptions that are happening. Think great, feel GREAT, and prepare to enhance your life.

# Chapter 2

# The Art of Letting Go

### Unconscious Success

I was asked why I believed that I survived the motorcycle accident. My first thought was of a higher power. Yet before I answered, I really thought about it: How did I survive, and with very little injuries? I replied, "It was because of the fact that I was knocked unconscious and was not able to control my fall or landing. I believe that if I were conscious, I would have been trying to catch myself, and I would have tensed up; and I would have broken a leg or an arm trying to catch myself."

I was successful in staying alive, by being unconscious: Unconscious Success.

Having learned that life happens for you and not to you, I wondered what the lesson was here. What can we learn from this? How many times do you end up losing your mind by trying to control everything, getting stressed out and frustrated?

Now, I am not saying that you should just let go of the steering wheel and just wish or hope that someone else will drive and take control. There is a balance between control and surrender. We do our best in controlling and managing our life: working hard, working smart, and taking action. Yet there are moments in life where we can no longer go on, knowing our capacity and our limits. "Limits?" you may ask. Well yes, to some extent. We don't know what we don't know. We are limited at times in our knowledge; thus, this is the reason we must continue to learn, and grow and expand our minds and our limits.

Our mind is like a muscle: we must continue to work it. An athlete will work out his or her muscles to a certain extent. Knowing how far they can push through, and while they can always push a little harder, they know that if they push too hard, a muscle can tear or an injury can occur. It is the same when we have reached that max point. There are some things in life that we cannot control. And that is okay. The universe works for us and not against us; just let go.

The Universe is leading us in the direction that we want to go, and we must trust the higher power. Our unconscious mind (or subconscious) has been programmed and conditioned to lead us in the right direction. Have you ever heard that we only use 10% of our brain? Well, I believe that we actually use all of it. It's just that a small percentage of information is processed by the conscious part of the brain—the part that does the critical thinking. The majority of information is processed by the unconscious mind. You don't have to remind yourself to breathe, or to blink every so often so your eyes don't dry out. You do this at the unconscious level.

Pay attention to where your attention is going. Energy flows where attention goes.

How do we self-talk to ourselves? What are we surrounding ourselves with—what things, people, places, etc.? How are we conditioning our mind? Is it with knowledge, or just with entertainment? While entertainment has its place, let's also keep learning and expanding our minds.

When was the last time we learned something new or achieved something that we had never achieved? How great did it feel to overcome and achieve it? Some of our greater memories are from when we were young, and we have these stories that we reminisce about. Yet if we really think about why those memories stand out, in most cases, it's because we learned something new, or overcame or achieved something, and we felt ALIVE. I believe that we can continue to learn, grow, expand, and evolve—and continue to feel alive.

When we stop learning or growing, we start dying, just like a tree. We must continue to nourish and feed our mind, spirit, and soul. We feed our bodies, yet we are more than just physical beings; we are spiritual beings as well.

## Stuck? Stop Holding On

Have you ever felt that you were stuck in a rut—in a boring routine—not knowing how to get out of it? I know I have been in a humdrum existence in the past. I had to ask myself what it was that I was holding on to. What was it about that circumstance that I had been attached to? What was the hidden benefit of doing the same thing over and over? It is like being in a relationship that is going nowhere: you argue, and you're angry and upset with each other, and yet you stay in this existence of misery. There is a quote that says, *"Better the devil you know than the devil you don't."* Honestly, that quote is for someone that is too scared of change: "Well, what if it gets worse?" Maybe ... IT WILL GET BETTER! Because we are learning from the current situation and will make wiser decisions in the future.

We feel stuck in many situations because we are not willing to let go—to let go of an idea, or the fact that we must be right and the other person is wrong; to let go of a grudge, or simply let go of our perception of that circumstance. I have a quote that I came up with, which helps me at times, and may help you as well. Remember to tell yourself: *"The quickest way to change any circumstance is to change my perspective."*

Holding on to a habit or situation means that we are in a comfort zone. We must break out of these comfort zones that are holding us back from moving forward in life. Let go!

Being in a comfort zone is comfortable, yet that means that you are settling for what you have or who you are in that moment. If you want more in life—more happiness, more love, more passion, and more romance—then it's time to do something new and get out of your comfort zone. There is more to who you are: you are a wonderful, amazing, and beautiful person, and you deserve more.

I was speaking with another speaker once, and he told me he believed in not stepping out of your comfort zone, but in expanding your comfort zone. Well, I believe, in order to expand your comfort zone, you must first step out of your boundaries, to conquer the unknown, and that's how you expand your comfort zone. The United States of America began because someone decided to sail the unknown ocean, find land, and conquer it. Then, after they were only 13 colonies, they still kept stepping over the boundaries to conquer and expand. As many countries have done this, we too must step out of our comfort zones on a continuous basis. Your success can only grow to the extent that you do.

Holding on and letting go is like breathing. We breathe in, slightly hold the breath, and then we exhale. They both work hand in hand. Yet some of us, in the past, have just held on, holding and holding and never letting go. It's like holding your breath until you're turning blue in the face and almost passing out. How many times has that happened to you? It's not until your life is seriously threatened that you let go, and you are able to breathe again. Hold on and let go.

*"If something or someone is meant to be in your life, you can let it go, and it will come back to you."* I also believe that sometimes you let go, and it, or they, might not even leave. It's like when we have a puppy on a leash, and we are afraid that if we take off the leash, he might run away, yet a lot of times it is just in our heads. We project and transfer our energy and feelings to the puppy, which gets him excited and all riled up. Just relax and let go, and take off the leash; and while in a calm and relaxed state, the puppy will also relax, and may just sit there or lie there. I believe that when we are relaxed, and

we trust the process and the universe, everything is going to be alright. Train the world around you to work with you, and be clear of your intentions and decisions of what you want in life.

## Give to Live

Giving is a form of letting go. Let go of some of the responsibilities that you have, and learn to GIVE some responsibility to someone else. A true leader will delegate responsibility, and will delegate some of those tasks to other people, employees, friends, or family. How many times have you tried to do everything yourself, because you feel that no one can do it as good as you can? We try to multi-task, and yet we end up half-assing most of our projects. We are not totally focused and present while doing these tasks, because we are already thinking of the next task or thing we need to do.

I have been guilty of trying to do everything myself as well. When I first bought the print shop, I was already the manager and graphic designer. I became the owner and still kept doing the same tasks. I was used to it and knew what the customers wanted. I hired my soon-to-be wife, Mireya, at the time, to take on some of the front office work, which helped me out immensely. A couple of years later, we upgraded our printers, from the old offset ones to digital printers, and our production guy, who ran these machines, decided to quit. He figured we didn't need him anymore, since he only knew how to work the old machines and not the new digital printers. Well, guess what I did? That's right... I took on the production as well. Then I was hardly able to work in my big office, since now I found myself in the back doing production. Two years passed, and I was still doing production. I was taking on something that I should have LET GO! We had also hired my step-son, Felix, which helped us in production, yet I had not given him more responsibility. I sat down with Felix and told him, "Felix, I think it is time I delegate more responsibility to you, and let you run the production department. We can also hire someone to help you with production." Felix agreed and said he was more than happy to do this, and then asked, "Of course, that means I'm getting a raise, right?" I smiled and said, "Yes, Felix, that means you get a raise."

Not everyone will do the task like you, and frankly, they don't have to. As long as they are willing to learn, and willing to continue to grow, they will improve. Not everyone is motivated by only money; some want to move up, have a goal that they can achieve, and be part of something great—not only for the company but also for their families, to show they are great providers and to feel proud of what they do.

It's like when you first get a new car; you are all excited, and you are driving it everywhere, and you feel great. Then, 10 years later, you are still in the same car; and maybe in 20 or 30 years, you are still in the same car. Wear and tear, and you are ready for a new one. You give that car away at a great deal, and the new person receiving it is excited about it, because it is new to them. You upgrade or get a different car, and you feel great again. Just in the same way, at work, you move into a new position; or you buy a new business, or you notice your business growing, or you close a new deal—and you FEEL GREAT! When we keep growing and moving up, whether it's in business or in life, we feel great and accomplished. Well, that goes for almost everyone. Therefore, when we are able to help those around us—co-workers, employees, business partners, friends or family—they will be grateful, and the universe will respond, and you will move up as well.

When you give, it doesn't have to be a tangible item. You can also give one of your most valuable things, and you might not even realize how precious it is: your time. We can always make money, yet we cannot get back our time. How do you spend time, and how do you share time? Are you fully present in the moment you give your time? How are you investing your time? Is it an expense or an asset? Are you wasting time or buying time? You want to live? Give time to your people. You are not in the real estate business, car business, insurance business, or printing business. You are in the people business. We should always be investing our time in people. It's not about competing with people; it's about collaborating with people. Help others, and karma will give it back to you. At times, it is those you assist that will return the favor. Other times, karma will pay it forward through another source. It's the law of reciprocation. Give.

You see, as you give, the Universe will give you something in return. Be a great receiver as well: great at giving, great at receiving; great at living, great at achieving.

Give with love and generosity, and you will receive likewise. When you can give genuinely, you can let go and not worry about the return. Because you are no longer thinking of yourself, you are thinking, "If I'm not giving, I am being of disservice to the other person that is waiting to receive." It's like we are all running in this relay race together. We grab the baton, run hard, giving it all we got, and we pass it on. It's a different race every day: different goals, give everything you have, and pass it on. Learn and share your knowledge. When you cannot give the baton away, then you cannot receive anything else the universe is trying to hand you, because there is something that you are still holding on to. When you make the space, the universe will fill it. By giving, you free your hands and make space to receive new things into your life.

## Lose Control

Letting go of control has many benefits. The conscious mind can only think of seven things at one time, plus or minus two. It is documented that our conscious mind makes up 0.006% of the mind, and the other 99.994% is our unconscious mind. While your conscious mind can only handle about 126 bits per second, your unconscious mind handles about 2.3 million bits per second every day. Your unconscious mind is the area or territory owned by your emotions. This is where your memories and learnings are. The unconscious mind preserves all your habits, knowledge gained, and perceptions.

Your mind is like a major corporation, and the CEO is your conscious mind, giving orders and commands. Your unconscious mind is all the other workers and employees, handling all the other tasks behind the scenes that makes it possible to make the CEO's command a reality.

There are many things that you do every day that are controlled by your unconscious mind, like breathing. You don't have to consciously think about it every second. Driving has become a habit for most; you do it so much that it is just a habit. You are driving, and you start thinking about your day, or something you need to take care of later, and your mind drifts, and you wonder how you have been driving the last 5 minutes. You ask yourself, "How did I make it through those last few traffic lights?" Your unconscious mind has formed a habit and generalized that all red lights mean stop, and all green lights means go, and you are driving unconsciously. There are things that you learn and keep doing until your conscious mind (the CEO) delegates and assigns the task to your unconscious mind; therefore, letting go of that task, letting go of control, and not micromanaging. There are many small business owners that stay small and are not able to grow their business because of not delegating those tasks, and not letting go of control. Similarly, many parents are afraid to give their kids responsibility, and are afraid that they will mess things up; and those parents just end up doing everything for their children, and they never grow up.

My wife tells me how her mother did not have the patience to teach her how to cook, and was afraid that she would burn the food or simply not do it right. My wife did learn to cook because her godmother had the patience and taught her, and she was able to let go and give her the time and responsibility to cook. My wife now cooks these amazing meals, and not just Mexican meals every day, but a variety of foods. My mother-in-law still thinks my wife can't cook, because it is not Mexican food, LOL. My wife cooks a lot of vegetables and healthy foods. My father-in-law once told my wife, "I'm not a rabbit; I can't even get full on this food."

When we are able to let go and delegate, some people may ask you why you don't just handle those things by yourself. Not everyone will agree with your new habits and new methods of handling life, yet when they begin to see the results and success you are having in your life, they might ask you, "How have you obtained more success in your life?" You can remind them: "Remember when you asked me, 'Why don't you just do it yourself?' Well, I started to delegate, and now I have more time to focus on the things that I enjoy doing."

Let go of who you are! Albert Einstein once said that we are not able to solve a problem with the same mind that created the problem. When you let go of your old ways of thinking, by learning new things and viewing things differently, you end up looking at your circumstances from a different perspective.

## Surrender

Let go of who you think you are and who you've told yourself you are. In order to let go of those memories that remind you of your past and who you are, you must surrender. What does the word, *surrender*, mean to you? According to Webster's dictionary, *surrender* means: an agreement to stop fighting, hiding, resisting, etc., because you know that you will not win or succeed; an act of **surrendering**: the act of giving the control or use of something to someone else; the act of allowing yourself to be influenced or controlled by someone or something.

*Art C. Guerrero*

There are moments when we just have to stop fighting with ourselves. I have heard it, seen it, and experienced it in many things. We try really hard to make something work, and it just doesn't happen for us, no matter how hard we make the effort. I've learned that maybe it's because it's not meant to happen. The Universe and/or God is trying to tell us there is something better for us. Stop fighting and stop resisting. What we resist only persists. For example, if you put your hand up, and I put my hand against your hand and push against your hand without really telling you anything or why, you will more than likely push back and create resistance. The harder I push, the more you will push back, especially if it's to the point of knocking you over. What we push, pushes back. Instead of resisting and pushing away from what we don't want, we need to grab hold of what we want—a thing, an idea, a dream, or a goal—and pull ourselves toward it.

Surrender is not always necessary, yet it's about knowing when it's time to move on to the next thing, and not keep hitting our heads on the wall. We are not always meant to succeed or win at everything all the time. Even in sports, nobody wins all the time. Similar to sports, in the game of life, it takes a team to win; one person alone does not win championships. Remember to have a team around you—friends, family, and co-workers—to help each other win in the game of life. In sports, when a player is badly injured, he doesn't keep playing with a broken leg; he surrenders and delegates, giving the control or opportunity to someone else to take over the responsibility. Surrender is not a bad thing; it's knowing when it's time to let someone else take over.

## Trust

Allowing yourself to be influenced or controlled by someone or something is not always easy; it takes trust and faith. The first person you should have trust and faith in is yourself, believing and having the confidence in yourself that you will make great choices in the people that you surround yourself with: a team that supports you and encourages you, and is there to lift and inspire you to move forward. Trust your gut feeling, your mind, and your heart on the decisions you make. A great leader will delegate, and will trust that the task that has been assigned will be completed.

I once saw a documentary about a weight loss program and how the individuals did very well following the program. In part two of the documentary, they followed up to see where these individuals were in the progress. We came to find out that one individual had been very successful in keeping off the weight, and the other had fallen back to his old habits and regained the weight. The difference was that one of them had a team of supporters, and the other did not have any supporters. This reminded me of a camping trip I took with my stepson, and there was an analogy that I used to explain how we need a team of supporters.

We were on the top of the hill, with a very nice view, instead of being in the valley by the river. It began to get very windy, and I noticed, as the wind began to pick up, our tent began to sway back and forth. I said, "Felix, you notice how that smaller tent at the campsite next to us is not moving as much as ours? Well, it's because it's a smaller tent, and it really only needs the four stakes supporting it. Our tent is a bigger tent, and it requires more stakes in the ground to support it, with rope pulling it from the top on all sides, holding it tight, so that the wind will not knock it over. Well, that is how our life is: We can stay small, and we will only need very few supporters. But if we decide to grow, and continue to get big in our endeavors or in business, we will need a team that supports us so that we will have a strong hold on things, to withstand anything that comes our way and tries to knock us down."

My son loved this analogy, and it made me think as well. Before we knew it, the wind got stronger, and a fierce gust pressed against the tent, and the tent snapped and fell to the ground. We looked at each other, and Felix was waiting for me to react or get upset. We still had one more night to camp, and now we had a broken tent. Then I remembered how a transformational speaker once told me, "Instead of getting upset and wondering why this happened to you, ask what you can learn from it. What is the lesson?" As I pondered, I asked Felix, "Why do you think the tent fell?" He looked back at me with a puzzled look, as if to say, "Well, because of the wind, of course." Yet before he could answer, I said, "Because the tent was not well supported, and in life, we must have strong-minded people and enough sponsors, and make sure that we have covered all our angles to ensure we stand strong." Felix absorbed this and agreed, "Wow ...makes sense."

Felix later said that he was surprised that I did not get mad because the tent broke. I smiled and replied, "There is no sense in getting upset; it doesn't solve anything to be upset or mad. We cannot think straight when we are upset. It is not the wind or the tent's fault; it is mine, since I did not make sure I had enough supporters to cover all the angles and secure the tent. We will figure out what to do about the tent later."

We can always rebuild and start over; it is not the end but the beginning of another chapter in life. Just remember to trust and have faith in yourself, in others, and in God or the Universe. Everything will work out, and everything is happening according to plan, even if it doesn't make sense at the time. The Universe will always align itself to your greatest desires and the bigger picture.

Life does not happen TO you, it happens FOR you. Trust.

# Chapter 3

# The Unknown and Its Wonders

**Comfort Zones**

Being creatures of habit, we like our routines. We usually wake up at the same time, eat the same thing for breakfast, or never eat breakfast, take the same route to work, and so on and so forth. Routines do have benefits, and having the discipline to follow your daily routine can be great to build a new habit. What happens in most cases is that we tend to stay on the same path for a long time, to the point that, before you know it, a year passes, and then five; and then ten years later, we wonder why nothing new has happened in our lives. Where did the time go? Why did we never advance in our career and in life? The definition for insanity is doing the same thing over and over, and expecting different results. We must push ourselves past our comfort zones. Sometimes we get very comfortable in our current situation, and we stay there. We are doing okay, and we adopt the saying, "If it isn't broke, don't fix it."

A friend I used to work with, when I was a teenager, showed up to work one day, but not in her car. I asked, "Dude, where's your car?" She replied in a disappointed tone, "Well, the engine in my car locked up, and there is no way to fix it. The mechanic said I should just get another car." I asked, "Why did the engine lock up on you?" She was embarrassed, and looked down and said, "Because I never changed the oil or checked the oil. I was running it with no oil." I couldn't believe my ears. I smiled and said, "Well, you're supposed to check and change the oil every 3 months or 3000 miles, whichever comes first!" "I didn't know, and no one ever told me." That's how life is: It might not be broken yet, but if we are not checking and changing the oil, and being proactive and doing maintenance, it might break down and leave you stranded. Just like no one told my friend to do the maintenance, many of us were not told to be proactive and continue to push ourselves. We are taught to go to school, go to college, be a good employee, and have a stable job and work there for 25 plus years. Know your position, and stay there until you retire.

Ken Courtright, who is a successful entrepreneur, has a podcast called, "Today's Growth: Growing Business Today," and has other successful businesses. In a training class, he said, "Any business that does not change anything in the way they run and do business, within 10–15 years, will fail 100% of the time." WOW!! That hit me like a ton of bricks and really made me think: "How am I running my business? Am I updating and staying current with what is changing in the world of business?" This also made me realize that this is true for other areas of life as well. As stated in the title of Cheri Huber's book, *"How you do anything is how you do everything."* Sometimes we have been in relationships where we stick to the same routines, and the relationship becomes a bit boring. With nothing new or exciting, it becomes predictable—not just with a significant other, but with friends, jobs, and careers. How many times have you noticed someone, from your hometown, who is still working at the same job they did when they were in high school? Some people are okay with that and are content, but if you are wanting to move forward and move up in your job, career, or life, you must continue to grow, learn something new, read a book, and study more about your career and field. Learn how to run a business you love.

Imagine you are in a room, with a padded folding chair, and you sit there comfortably relaxing. Yet once you realize that there is another door that leads to the next room, you get up to see what is in this room. You realize that there is a nice plush reclining chair. Then you take a look back at the folding chair where you were just sitting. Are you going to go back and sit in the folding chair? Or are you going to get your things and move to the next room, and sit in the nice plush reclining chair? Most people stay seated in the folding chair because they are used to the chair, and they are afraid to find out what is behind the other door, not knowing what to expect or if it will be worse. Will the door lock behind me? Will I have to sit on the floor and be uncomfortable? Maybe. Yet once you calm down, you realize there is another door in your life, and you move across this scary room and open that door, and you realize ...There is now a couch in that next room! Was it worth moving forward? Yes! While some people find it easier to stay in their comfort room, or comfort zones, it is the people that move across different rooms that find new rewards with every room they cross. Many that have been successful in their business, and in their lives, have had to cross a few scary and frightening rooms, yet have found success because of it. Will you take the risk and just go for it?! Only you can decide whether you will get out of your comfort zone and receive the many benefits and rewards that await you.

*Art C. Guerrero*

**The Power of Questions**

Embrace the unknown and its wonders. Be willing to ask questions. There is so much power in asking questions. I know you have heard the saying, "Knowledge is Power." Well, in order to gain more knowledge, we must ask questions. The more questions we ask, the more knowledge we gain. When we move past our comfort zone into unknown territory, we will have questions; yet if we are able to prepare ourselves by asking questions and are willing to learn, we will be better prepared. Then you might have another question, and that's okay. The thing is to keep asking questions and keep learning.

I once worked as a car salesman, at a car dealership, where I learned a quote that resonated with me: *"The one asking questions is the one in control of the conversation."* This makes sense, because the one asking questions is leading the conversation in the way they want it to go. I feel this is also true in life. As we ask questions, we lead our life in a direction, not only by asking other people questions, but also questioning ourselves: "Am I happy? "Is there more to this? Can I be doing something else to help my situation or to help someone else?" If we are not asking these questions, then someone else is asking us those questions; and they are leading us into a certain direction, which might not be the direction that we are wanting to go. This is also true in leadership. Someone is always leading, and someone is always following. You lead your family or your relationship. Is one person asking most of the questions, or is everyone participating in asking questions, equally, to ensure that the group is all going in the direction that everyone agrees on.

## The Art of Unconscious Success

At one time in my life, I remember being part of our church youth group. If only I had spoken up and asked more questions. Given my opinion on how things could have been done differently, we might have had a better outcome to the problem we were trying to resolve. Or the time where I was working at a job where I could have moved up and been promoted to a new position, yet because I did not ask the question, someone or something else led my life to a destination that I was not aiming for. *"A closed mouth doesn't get fed."* The first time I heard this was from my friend, Marcus Sauseda. Then, I later heard it from Cheryl Foston. The way Cheryl puts it, *"It means that if you don't ask for what you want, you can't expect to get it. Maybe you'll get what you want, or you may get shut down, but one thing is for sure, you will never know if you don't ask."* Therefore, speak up when you are hungry for knowledge, because if you don't, you will starve and die! (Metaphorically speaking, of course, because if we are not growing, learning, and evolving, we are dying.) Just like plants and trees, we need to keep watering and cultivating our lives, to not only breathe but to thrive and live to our full potential.

To formulate a question is something that is only displayed by humans. It shows a higher level of cognitive thinking, and higher intelligence to know that something is incomplete or left out, and therefore, we seek an answer and have the ability to create and ask a question. While the great ape can answer questions, we have never known the ape to ask a question. A key component to the questioning and artistic spirit is the idea of fragmentation. If you want to be on the cutting edge, and be original, you must be different. The tapeworm, when it breaks and fragments into two separate pieces, becomes two different individuals. The ants also show us that when there is another ant in front of it, it goes from leader to follower, and at times, it can cause these ants to go in circles forever until they die, unless there is one ant that breaks from its programming and steps out of formation, saving the colony.

If we look at human history, we find that it is those individuals that broke out of the norm, and were brave enough to be curious and inquisitive, and ask the questions that have changed and impacted our lives and the world. What would the world be like without the curious questions asked by Albert Einstein, Thomas Edison, Nikola Tesla, Benjamin Franklin, or Steve Jobs, whose Apple slogan advised us to *Think Different*.

To question, shows higher intelligence, and if only a human can formulate a question, know that we have been given a gift and have the *power to question*. While you must be a great student to be a great teacher, and a great follower to be a great leader, eventually you must take the knowledge you have acquired, break free, and become an individual, and lead your family, your relationship, your tribe, and your life. You have the power to question.

## Un-Learn & Re-Learn

As we ask new questions, we will acquire new information that will rewrite and replace the current information. In other words, we must unlearn and relearn.

## The Art of Unconscious Success

Once there was a master monk who asked his student, "Would you like more tea to drink?" The student said, "Yes," and the master began to pour and pour. The student noticed that the cup was almost full, and he told his master, "It is full." The master continued to pour as the tea began to overflow. He continued to pour, and the student put his hand in front of the cup and said, ENOUGH! The master monk said, "Like this cup, you are full of opinions and speculations. To see the light of wisdom, you must first empty your cup." (a scene in the movie, *2012*)

We want to learn new information and take on new ideas, yet at times have had difficulty letting go of the old ideas and beliefs. We have these ideas and beliefs that we learned and picked up from somewhere in our past, and most of them come from our childhood. We learned an idea or belief from a parent, a guardian, or teacher, and made it our own. Yet it is good to question and reanalyze if this idea or belief makes sense. Where did it originate from, and is this a reliable source, or have new studies and research proven this idea to be incorrect or different in some way? Once you have analyzed and re-evaluated, you can make up your own mind; you can choose to delete the old information and the old programming, and take on new beliefs, with more clarity, and make more sense of things.

Some individuals are not willing to update their computers to a new software or firmware, and I ask, "Why haven't you updated your computer?" And the most common answer is, "Well, I'm already used to it, and I don't want to relearn the program again." Many agree that our minds are like a computer, or vice versa; yet many of us are running on old programming, on old software. Sometimes our life freezes up or is running slow, and we feel stuck and frustrated with the way our life is running. Well, my friend, it is probably because we are still running on Windows 98, or Mac OS 9. When was the last time you updated your operating system, software, or your mind? We must uninstall the old and install the new. Unlearn and relearn.

Just as you learn something new and get used to it, you might just get an update notice. Be open and ready to get out of your comfort zone, and re-learn. And like our computers, we are constantly updating. Usually the update is something minor, or only a few things are changed; and therefore, there are only a few new things to learn. The longer we wait to update, the more changes that will pile up, and the more we will have to learn later when we finally decide to update. Why wait until we are forced to update because we can no longer run the program, or because our computer or our lives finally crash. Now we must seek help from a computer tech, life coach, counselor, or mentor to help us fix and reboot our life. It's a good idea to have these guardians in our lives, to maintain and make sure we are running our operating systems, and our lives, smoothly.

Just as we unlearn, it is great to unplug. We are running our lives so fast, and like some people, we forget to reboot our phones, and our phones freeze up or crash—Dang! When was the last time we rebooted our phones? ...our computers? ...our lives? Unplug and take a vacation, or even take time to just sit in silence without all the noise. This is why I believe that meditation is a very healthy practice. Greg Montana, who is known as the Quantum Monk who studied quantum physics, told me once that even our mind is noisy, and to meditate is to quiet down the mind chatter and to sit in the stillness. Being in a state of awareness, we will find enlightenment. I believe that doing daily meditations is a great way to reboot our mind on a daily basis. Many have noticed a great change in how they operate on a daily basis, with much more clarity and peace, and on a higher energy level.

Be willing to unlearn and relearn new ideas. This is a necessary process to be able to evolve and continue to grow and expand your horizons. Consistently update and upgrade, and stay current and up-to-date on what is going on in the world around you. Unlearn and delete anything in your life that is no longer of any use or is not serving you in any way. Always remember to continuously save the new changes, and occasionally, REFRESH!

## Blank Canvas

When we refresh, we get a fresh start to a new day in our new life. Today is the first day of the rest of your life. We have heard this before, yet I feel, every morning, with meditation, I'm hitting the refresh button and starting my day clear-headed, with a smile on my face, ready to start my day. Sometimes when we update or upgrade, it is like starting from a blank canvas. When we unlearn and clear everything, it can be a great start to a new beginning  No longer looking at the same old picture, we get to create a new picture, and maybe a more colorful and vivid painting: a new picture of our lives.

I recall one very specific day in art class, when I was about to begin a new painting, and I just stared at my blank canvas for about five minutes. Well, my teacher, Mrs. Underwood, came up to me and said,

"Well, get to it; start painting already!" I smiled, looked up at her, and said, "I have already begun; I am painting the images with my mind, and arranging it in the way that I wish. Once I am satisfied with my arrangement, and the colors are to my liking, I will then just trace the picture that my mind has already laid out." She looked at me, and said, "Okay then, I'll leave you to it."

Similarly, I began to design my life with visualization, a different way of meditation; not just clearing your mind, which is great at times, but to create and imagine the future I wanted. Just as I did in art class, I imagined the infinite possibilities, and I began to design with my thoughts, and create my reality of the future I wanted. I was imagining vividly, with all my senses, what it looks like and what it sounds like. What aromas do I smell; what can I feel emotionally, and what can I physically touch or taste? I've come to understand that if you can imagine a reality, then that reality does exist, because you created it by imagining it. Therefore, once I create and visit this new reality, and experience it vividly, knowing this reality exists, I begin to reverse engineer it. If this reality is five years from now, I move backwards in time, closer to the present, and ask what three years would look like. What would two years be like; then, where would I be one year from now, and then nine months, ...six months, ...three months, ...30 days, ...two weeks, and what would I need to be and do a week from now? What needs to happen a week from now for me to be on track to the new reality I want to reach? I write down these steps and these goals that I must complete to be on track.

Now, once you decide to experience this type of meditation, and you continue to visit this reality, feel free to adjust anything you would like to fine-tune on your long-term goal and reality. As you continue to visit this memory of the future, your mind will imagine it, and your body will experience it. You will begin to accept this as a real experience, and you will reach your desired destination. Scientists have proven that an athlete's brain fires off the same neuro connections when they imagine they are running, and when they are actually running. The unconscious mind cannot tell the difference between what is actually physically happening or being imagined.

Therefore, by imagining and experiencing a future reality or future memory, your brain will begin to rewire itself to accommodate this new reality, and the more we meditate on this, the more the brain continues to hardwire this reality. Nerves that fire together, wire together. The Universe will begin to align itself to what you are wanting and aiming for.

The world and our reality that we presently see and experience, is a world that our mind is creating by our present perspective and how we decide to feel about it emotionally. We cannot change anyone else; the things we have control over, and the power to change, are our thoughts, perceptions, and actions. I remind myself, "The quickest way to change any circumstance is to change my perspective."

The blank canvas concept is a great way to create the future you want. For any present circumstance, we can re-evaluate, and change our perspective and how we feel about it. Instead of living from our memories of the past, we can bring those memories into our present. Let's live a new life from a future present reality, from creating and remembering your future memories.

(Visit ucsuccess.com to download your free copy of *U.C. Success Meditation* audio file.)

## Embrace NEWness

Welcome the unknown. Some say they wish they knew the future and what will happen. But where would the fun be in that? We are curious creatures. We like to be surprised, and to discover new things. We love watching movies where we do not know what will happen in the plot. If it is too predictable, we don't rate it as a good movie. It has to have twists and turns, and really surprise us, to be an excellent film.

It's good to look at life like a movie, and where you are the main character, producer, and director. You don't really want to live a life that is predictable and boring, where sometimes you find your life in the same rut, in the same routine, on that same hamster wheel, do you?!

I've witnessed relationships fall apart because there was never anything NEW in the relationship. It was always the same thing, day in and day out. I've asked couples, "When was the last time you guys went on a date, or did something out of the ordinary—something NEW? Even on a regular day, nothing special, just to say I love you?" In my up and coming book on relationships, *The Art of Magical Relationships*, I speak of love, and how you must first love yourself and value yourself so that your partner will do the same. We teach others how to treat us, by how we treat ourselves. Do something out of the ordinary, and surprise yourself with new and different things—not *try*, but *do* NEW things. Learn a NEW instrument, pick up a NEW hobby—do it for yourself, and your loved ones will want to join you. They will be inspired to learn or do something different for themselves. People will say to you, "Wow! I did not know you could do that!" Well, neither did I, and neither will you unless you embrace newness.

If someone was giving you something, would you prefer a used item or a used gift, or a brand-spanking-new gift? The NEW one of course. While I was grateful to receive my cousin's hand-me-downs (used clothes) and wear them when I was a child, I truly enjoyed receiving NEW clothes and NEW toys, and showed an immense gratitude.

We like the certainty that something works; since someone else was using it, we know that it works. I've purchased motorcycles that were used and were daily riders. I knew, because they were being used on a daily basis, the maintenance was kept up. Similarly, we enjoy watching the same movies over again, even though we have already seen them; yet we hope that it has been long enough that we don't remember everything that will happen, so that we will still be surprised. We can model people and what they have done, and what is working for them, yet it is those that are willing to do something NEW that stand out. What is it that no one else has attempted or done, that will be NEW and cutting edge?

Something NEW will always continue to happen, whether we make it happen or someone else does. NEW things happen every day, and NEW things are being discovered. We must be willing to stay open and embrace NEW technologies, NEW ideas, NEW discoveries, NEW programs, NEW apps, and NEW ways of doing things.

My wife and I own a print shop and, at times, we have customers that want invitations for a wedding, and they are usually looking for the old-fashioned style, with embossed images, foil lettering, and ribbons. While those are nice, we advise that we create the more modern styles, in full color, which have a quicker turnaround time and a reasonable price. We show them a few samples and explain why most of our customers have switched and gone to a more modern and NEW look. We are able to enlighten our customers, and most of them get a modern style of invitation. Most of our customers that are looking for invitations, say that every other print shop said, "No, we don't make those;" yet no one was explaining why they didn't make those, or explain to them why the modern ones were the way to go, to be up-to-date and embrace the NEW style. I believe that, many times, we continue to use the same method of doing things because no one has really shown or explained to us a NEW way. Instead of waiting for someone else to show you a NEW way, discover a NEW way for yourself. When you discover a NEW way, you enter a NEW realm and a NEW reality, and you will discover many NEW wonders. You enter into a state of euphoria as you reach your goals and reach NEW fortunes, which will fuel and propel you toward NEW goals and NEW success.

I have noticed many successes in my life due to the fact that instead of fighting or resisting change, I accept and adapt to NEW ideas, and change my perspective on things.

I once heard some kids (a brother and sister) saying, "That's weird!" I smiled and told them, "It is not weird; it's just NEW to you." The older sister looked at me, and said, "Yes, that makes sense." She would later repeat that to her younger brother anytime he would say, "That's weird!"

Once we learn to embrace the weirdness—the newness—it will change our perspective on life, and thus change the world around us.

**Do Something Different**

We are not perfect. Sometimes we may make mistakes and fail at something we are attempting to accomplish. If at first you don't succeed... What? .... Try and try again? Ehhhh!! WRONG. "Why?" you may ask. First off, the word, *try*, means to attempt something. There is no *try*—either you do it or don't do it. Second, if you just keeping doing the same thing, you will keep getting the same results. You have heard the definition of insanity: to keep doing the same thing over and over again, and expecting different results. Therefore, if at first you don't succeed, you go about it in different way, and if that doesn't work, you do it from another approach. Do something different. You have a goal, and you go for it; you might just have to take a different path to get there. Take a detour. It might take you a bit longer, but you will eventually get to your destination and accomplish your goals.

There are certain paths that the Universe and/or God will lead us through, and we may want to take shortcuts to get to our destination. Yet the path is designed a certain way, with obstacles for us to learn from, and this way, we are more prepared once we reach our destination. It is when we reach an obstacle that we may struggle to get through, and we may want to avoid that obstacle, but it might be our approach that we may need to adjust—to look at things differently, from a different angle, and do different things until we successfully overcome the obstacle.

I once did a *Tough Mudder* run, which was 12 miles long, with 25 obstacles I had to overcome to finish the run successfully. It was definitely a challenge, and once our team reached the finish line, it was an amazing feeling of accomplishment to finish that course. There were times when I looked at an obstacle as a huge challenge, and I had to take a deep breath and look at different ways to approach that obstacle, and if one way didn't work, I did something different.

At our print shop, sometimes we get a paper jam on our printers. Sometimes we just remove the paper jam and hit start, and we get another jam and other jam. I remind my employees, and myself, that it's okay, and that we can do something different. There is a reason we continue to get this paper jam. Let's look at our options: Is the paper too thick, and we need to adjust the paper settings on our printer? Or is the paper too big, and we need to adjust the speed, and slow down the paper as it feeds through the printer? Or if the paper will not feed correctly from the tray, do we need to adjust the feed rollers, by tightening or loosening? Let's do something different. There is a reason why the jam is happening, and it's usually not printer error but user error. How often does that show up in our lives, where we are blaming someone or something else? *Aw, this machine doesn't work, or that car doesn't work.* Maybe, we didn't service it or change the oil, or we have been running it wrong, and that is why it is not working.

We sometimes do this in relationships, where we blame our partner or spouse, and we wish them to be different. Well, have you done something different yourself; looked at it differently or changed your way of doing things? You chose that partner or spouse. When you do something different and change your approach, you will get different results in your business and personal life. Don't get hung up on just one way of doing things in life, or even doing things the way everyone else does. Do something different, and push through with courage and confidence. With every obstacle you overcome, you will continue to gain more confidence. There will be some obstacles that may seem small to you or insignificant; yet they are still accomplishments and goals reached. Even if they are small goals, celebrate the victory; celebrate every success. This also programs your unconscious mind to celebrate and attract more wins and success to your life.

Doing something different or doing things differently will get your mind thinking more creatively, and you will begin to be more resourceful. Some believe that they are not creative or artistic. Being artistic is just another way of saying you are creative. We all have creativity, yet some of us practice it more than others. To become more artistic or creative is to continue to be resourceful and figure out different ways to do things. By making this a habit, your unconscious mind will program itself to continuously view life from different angles. Think differently, and do something different.

# Chapter 4

# The Power of Choice

**Everything is Choice**

Everything is *choice*. You either choose to believe you have the choice, or you choose not to. Either way, you choose. For example, you choose to get up early, or you choose to hit the snooze button (and some of us hit it five times before we get up). The *snooze button*: Whose idea was it to create that? You have all heard the saying, *"You snooze, you lose,"* yet it's on your alarm clock.

Choose wisely, and get up; your new life is waiting for you. Today is the first day of the rest of your life. Be awake, and be aware that you are AWARE. We are the only species that is consciously aware of itself. We tend look at our actions, analyze, and choose to imagine what would, could, or should happen. We get stuck in our lives when we get *paralysis by analysis*. When you get to a crossroad, you want to make a quick choice. We have more than just our mind to make a choice; we have our gut feeling and our heart. Most are not aware that our heart can think, feel, and choose for itself. There are around 40,000 neurons—an entire network of neurotransmitters—in the heart. We will cover more on the heart and mind, in Chapter 8. Just know that we have more than just our minds to make a choice.

Before we go any further, let's talk about the difference between *decisions* and *choices*. According to the dictionary, the definitions are as follows:

> **Decision**: the act of, or need for, making up one's mind.
> **Choice**: the right, power, or opportunity to choose.

When we look at the origins of the words, *decision* comes from *cutting off*, and *choice* comes from *to perceive*. Taking a look at this closer, we can gain some clarity.

With decisions, we go through a process and analysis of elimination or cutting off options. With choice, the approach is based more on a mindset. We have a perception of what is right and wrong. You make choices based on your beliefs and values. What is aligned with your core beliefs? With this said, when you know what your goals are, when you have a mission, a vision, and a clear view of what you want your future to be, it makes it easier to choose. Ask yourself: "Is this choice aligned with my mission, my vision, and with my goals?"

Getting clear on your goals, will help you in making choices quickly and moving forward toward your goals.

Another way that I have looked at the difference, is that a decision is like going to a shoe store: You have many options, and it is taking a long time to decide. Why? Because you are overloaded with too many options. When you break it down to only two options, and now you only have two choices—brown shoes or black shoes—you are now making a choice: this or that? In sales, this is great, because you are only giving a customer two choices—none of which has the option of saying no. In neuro-linguistic programming, or NLP, this is called a *double bind*. I mention this is great for sales, yet this is great in life as well, because you are your own salesperson. You sell yourself on ideas every day. If you are not selling yourself, someone else is selling you on their idea. Choices are very similar.

If we do not make a choice, someone else will make the choice for us.

One of the greatest abilities that most entrepreneurs and millionaires have is to make a choice quickly and take action. Listen to your inner voice, and decide. You can research to make an educated decision, yet you have already learned and gained knowledge along the way, and if you are brought to this crossroad, it is because the Universe (or God) believes that you are ready to make the choice. We are all doing the best we can, with the skills and knowledge we have at this moment in time. *Ready, fire, aim*—I know, you're thinking, it's *ready, aim, fire*. Too many times, we are sitting there, overthinking our aim, and taking too long or never firing, because we are not sure if we are going to hit our target. Just FIRE, and once you see where it hits on the target, you know how far and how much to correct, so keep firing until you hit the target. Now that you have made the choice to fire, the next time, you will have more confidence, and you will get better at firing and at making choices.

## Anything is Possible

To obtain the power of choice, you must first believe that anything is possible. Realize that the world around you exists due to the fact that you have created it. You have made the conscious or unconscious decision to keep certain things and people in your life. Either way, you choose this reality. Some choices and decisions you make are based on unconscious programming that you are running in your mind and making choices on autopilot. For example, when you go to the refrigerator, and you are trying to decide between apple pie and pecan pie, you believe you consciously made the decision, yet your unconscious mind has a memory of when you were young, and your grandmother used to make her famous apple pie, and you remember how happy you were to sit down with your grandma and laugh at her jokes as you both ate apple pie together. There is a memory anchored to apple pie and, therefore, you choose apple pie unconsciously, believing that it's just what you felt like that day, when in actuality, there is a deeper reason.

Just like the apple pie example, most of us are making choices unconsciously, and we choose apple pie because it is familiar. You make most of your choices based on a memory of the past. As we have learned, the more you keep doing what you have been doing, the more of the same you will keep getting. When you can make a choice based on a memory of the future, based on the end goal, you are moving forward and toward your goals. Take for example, an excellent chess player, who is not only looking at the current move but making the conscious choice of playing five moves ahead, or even more. The current choice might not make sense to some, because they are not looking ahead. We do things today that most people won't, so that tomorrow we can do things that most people can't. Sometimes you have to sacrifice a pawn.

"If you want to make an omelet, you have to break some eggs."

Anything is possible. The only limits you have are the ones that you put in front of yourself; the ones you create. If you think you can, you can; if you think you cannot, then you cannot. Either way, you are right.

Have you been in a situation where you felt that you had no choice? The hard truth is that you always have a choice. But is it based on a belief or value, or on who you think you are? You choose not to go against certain beliefs and values. You believe, based on who you are, that you must make a choice or decision in a certain way. Yet when you look at things from a third person point of view, you are able to look at things without being attached or having a biased opinion. When you can see things for what they truly are, you can make an educated choice. You are able to make choices based on your own experience, versus being based on someone else's experience. The choice truly becomes your choice, without influence.

*"In every moment of our existence, we are in that field of all possibilities, where we have access to infinite choices."*
– Deepak Chopra

A possibility is a reality that exists, and therefore, there are infinite realities. When someone says, "If you do this, then this will happen," that is only one possibility, and there could be a likelihood that the same outcome may occur as before; yet it is also up to the person to believe in a different outcome. Take the example of the four-minute mile: For many years, no one believed that it was possible for humans to run the mile in under four minutes. Many believed, including scientists, that it was impossible, until 1954, when Roger Bannister broke the record. Within a year, so did 24 others. Now, over 1400 people have ran the mile in under four minutes. Everything is impossible until someone does it, and then it becomes possible. How great is it when you get to be the first ever to accomplish something that no one has ever done before?

Set new records and new standards; raise the bar. Do something that no one else has done before. Become the leader in your field, your career, your family, and in your life. The possibilities are endless. When you can imagine any possibility, your choices are endless.

## Become Someone Else

*"In order to do something you've never done, you've got to become someone you've never been. I think that all of us have great potential within us, but greatness is a choice; it's not our destiny. And in the pursuit of our dreams, we are introduced to trials, failures, and disappointments, which take us to the door of discovery and greatness."* – Les Brown.

Becoming someone else, and the things you can accomplish, are infinite. The person with the most flexibility will always overcome and have more choices, and therefore, have the most influence in any situation. When what you are doing is not working, do something different.

Imagine yourself as someone else, walking in someone else's shoes, and from a new perspective; you will be able to feel and think differently about a situation or circumstance, thus making it possible to choose different choices. If you had been been raised in a different country, a different culture, or maybe even just a different city, you might have grown into a different person. With different surroundings and experiences, you would adopt different beliefs and values. Changing your environment and behaviors is something you can change consciously and with much more awareness. When you are able to look into your unconscious mind, you can look at the deeper levels, and your beliefs, values, and identity. When you choose to change your identity and become someone else, you must also change your beliefs and values. You don't have to change all of your beliefs; just those that are not allowing you to achieve your dreams and goals. Believe that you can be financially free. If you want to have wealth and achieve more, don't just WANT to, but also BELIEVE that you can achieve your goals and have success.

I've discussed with my father, who is also a preacher, about the interpretation of the Bible scripture, in Mark Chapter 5, which talks about the woman who believed if she could only get through the crowd and touch the clothes of Jesus, she would be healed. When she did, she was immediately healed, and Jesus asked, "Who touched me?" Then the woman spoke up and told Jesus that it was her. He said, "Your faith has healed you." It was not that Jesus healed her, for he was asking, "Who touched me?" It was her FAITH—her belief that she would be healed.

When you can analyze and ask yourself, "Are those my beliefs and values, or are those someone else's that I took on and made my own? What do we truly value?" And when you are able to look at what resonates with you, you will begin to feel whole and more connected with your true self. What makes someone else happy will not necessarily make you happy.

When you can strip away all the layers, you will find the core of your true self. When you can be no one—without the titles, without ethnicity, from nowhere, no place, and nothing—it is then and at that place that you can connect with your spirit, your higher self, and be connected with source. From there, you can start to build toward being something, from somewhere to someone, and then be connected to everything, to everywhere, and to anyone. The moment where you have the power of choice, you can choose who you want to become at any given point in time.

On the next page is the common diagram of the iceberg-model of the mind. This is how most view the conscious mind and the unconscious mind. Now, looking at the seven layers of the mind from this standpoint, you can see why many believe that we are a product of our environment.

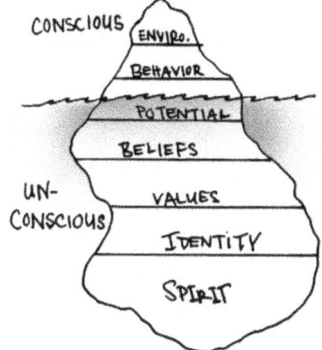
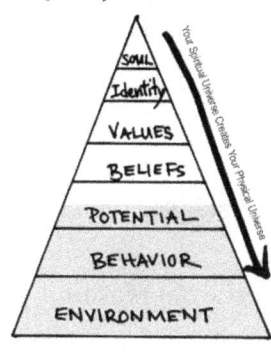

Illustration by: Art C. Guerrero

(Visit ucsuccess.com to download PDF copy of illustration and *Seven Layers of the Mind explained* word doc.)

In the seven layers of the mind or consciousness, spirit is at the top, and is one that few reach to connect with. Next, we work down toward identity—the *I am* statement.

When someone is asked, "Who are you?" many reply with what they do for a living: a doctor, a teacher, a fireman, etc. Yet when you truly look at WHY you are doing what you do for a living, you will know who you truly are and why you do what you do.

When you ask someone, "Who are you?" and if you notice their body language, they will usually place their hand on their chest and say, "I am _____." Now notice that if we are placing our hand on our chest, then we could say that we are placing our hand over our heart, instead of our head. This is because, when we are choosing an identity, we start from our spirit, and the best way to connect to our spirit is to connect through our heart.

## How to Decide

How do you make up your mind? With your heart. The heart connects us to the spiritual universe, which creates our physical universe. "How so?" you may ask. If you look at the first verse of the bible, it says: *"In the beginning, God created heaven and earth."* Another way of saying this is that the spiritual universe created the physical universe. It does not say that the earth created the earth. Many times, we try to use something physical to resolve an issue in the physical universe. Then we wonder why the issue has only temporarily been resolved instead of permanently. Sometimes we are only masking the issue. Similarly to taking medicine to make us better, it only temporarily relieves the symptoms.

Our heart is connected to the spiritual universe, more than the mind. There have been studies done, and scientists have discovered that the heart puts out more energy and reaches further. This is why scientists say that a mother can sense when her child is in danger, even if they are on the other side of the world. This also happens in twins. In the spiritual universe, there is no space and no time. We are taught in the physical universe that to travel a certain distance, it will take a certain amount of time. Yet when there is no space, then we can get there in no time.

When we make a choice—with our heart, full conviction, and faith—and we are determined, things will usually happen the way we want. The times that it does not happen for us is because we have other limiting beliefs that contradict what we want. It is those little doubts in the back of the mind that tell us we cannot do it, or that we are not good enough. This is why I say that we must have full conviction and faith.

One day, there was an event that my wife and I attended, and at the reception dinner table, we had a couple of seats available. A young lady and her friend sat down, since our table was the only place where seats were available. We talked for a while, and the young lady ended up telling us that she BELIEVED that she was not pretty, and she had low self-esteem because of it. My wife told her that she was beautiful, and that it would be wise to look in the mirror every morning, and say, "I am beautiful; I am beautiful; I am beautiful," and I agreed. Then she said, "Even if I don't believe it?" The way that she said it... *even if she did not believe it?* Huh? This made me think and realize that this is why affirmations usually don't work. You must believe it with all your heart. Do not just think you are—know you are. To know that something will happen for you, means you believe it with all your heart, because you have faith. Faith is what gives you confidence—knowing beyond a shadow of a doubt.

Through your heart, you connect to spirit, believing in yourself (identity) that anything is possible. Through faith, it changes your beliefs, which changes your behavior and attitude about yourself and the world around you, thus changing your environment (your physical universe).

Listen to your heart—your intuition—and you will be able to make choices that will lead you to the life that you truly want, with happiness, joy, confidence, and love, without having fear or being unsure if you have made the right choice. When you are able to make a choice connected to spirit and knowing who you are, you are making the best choice possible. You are making the best choice with the skills and knowledge that you have at this point in time. Some will say, "In retrospect, I would have made a different choice." Of course, you would have, because you are now a different person, who has acquired new skills and knowledge along the way.

A friend of mine, Ken Courtright, said, "When you read a book, highlight those things that jump out at you. Then read it again, six months or a year later, and highlight the most interesting things again. I bet that you will highlight different things." This is because you have learned new skills and knowledge, and you are looking at life through a different point of view. This is true with movies as well: When you see a movie again, you will catch different things that you did not notice before.

Remember to stay connected with your heart and soul. When you make a choice, it is not always about right or wrong, or whether it makes sense; sometimes the question you must ask is, "Does it feel right?"

## The Power of Intention

An important thing that you must look at, when making choices, is to ask yourself what your intention is. This plays a major role in what you create in your life, whether you know consciously or unconsciously. The power of intention is amazing, because intention comes from the spiritual universe, which manifests your physical universe. When you look at the word, *intention*, and its origin, intention means *purpose, design, or aim*. What is your purpose when making a choice? What is the desired outcome that you are looking for? What is your aim? When we have an intention, we have something to aim for. If you don't have a goal or dream, there's nothing to aim at, and that's why you hit nothing. I remember a time when one of my intentions was short-term gratification. I really wanted something *now*, and I would buy it *now*. Then, next month, I would be short on my rent or car payment. I had to really analyze my intentions, and look at things from a different point of view. I began to manage my finances from a more intelligent point of view. Expense or asset? Will this purchase make me money or not?

Find out what intentions you have that are serving you, and what intentions you must change to see the results that you want in your life.

Intention creates ideas that we assume or claim as true, thus creating a certain point of view. It is your point of view that creates your perception of the physical universe that you call your reality. Yet it is still being viewed through your mind's eye. This is the reason your point of view is different from others.

My wife and I went to a concert once, and when someone asked how she liked the show, she said, "Eh, it was okay." And I said, "It was awesome!" Why does this happen? We experienced the same show, and sat right next to each other, yet we both had two different points of view, and different opinions about the show. She said it was not loud enough, and the singer was a little off key, and it could have been done better. For me, I enjoyed all the songs, and the light show and performance was spectacular! My intention while at the show was to enjoy the show and spend time with my wife. For my wife, her intention was to see how good the band really played and sounded. Her intention created that point of view of her experience.

Intention is a force in the Universe that allows the act of creation to take place. Therefore, be aware and mindful of your intentions, and you will be aware of the creations you create in your reality.

Once you connect with your heart, soul, and your intention, you will have the clarity to make a choice with more ease, knowing that your choice is aligned with your heart and serves your purpose and intention, as well as your mission and vision.

**Take Action**

Move forward in bringing your dreams to life, and create your physical universe. There will be moments that the spiritual universe will manifest opportunities; knowing that you have requested and claimed a certain existence to be true, you will have created a postulate.

(Postulate definition: suggest or assume the existence, fact, or truth of (something), as a basis for reasoning, discussion, or belief.)

When the opportunity presents itself, TAKE ACTION. I once heard that the more open you are, the more opportunities you will have. I finally came to realize exactly what this meant. It's because the more open-minded I was in seeing someone else's point of view, the more my point of view would expand; understanding their point of view, but not necessarily adopting their point of view—just understanding why they believed and viewed the world as they do.

When connecting with others, you want to connect with OQP (Only Quality People). The brain of an intelligent person has fewer neuro connections, but *"the assumption has been that larger brains contain more neurons and, consequently, possess more computational power,"* Erhan Genç, a researcher at Ruhr-University Bochum, mentioned in a news release. Research has shown that the brains of the most intelligent individuals have less neuronal activity during test-taking than those of less intelligent individuals. *"Intelligent brains possess lean, yet efficient neuronal connections,"* concludes Genç. *"Thus, they boast high mental performance at low neuronal activity."*

When we have only quality people in our lives, who are connected with our purpose and intention, there is no guessing and having to look at all the noise of information. Nowadays, on the internet and social media, there is so much information that it confuses and clouds people's judgement. When we are not connected with our soul and spirit, we are not aware of our intentions or purpose. We are digging through all the noise, searching all over the brain, and making unnecessary connections. When we throw away ideas and information that do not serve us, we will have more defined and stronger neuro connections. Have stronger relationships, by no longer having old relationships that no longer serve you. Just like the brain, the more you connect with quality people, the stronger the connection becomes, and the weaker the other nerve fiber becomes, and the less it will present itself. Those old friends, by themselves, will fade away because, as you grow and become a new person, they will no longer have anything in common with you and will not be able to relate.

A large part in making choices is to take action! Be quick to take action because the window of opportunity will close before you know it. Take, for example, how three different people could have an idea of a new product or invention that they came up with. They could be from different parts of the world, but it is the one that files the patent first that will have the rights to the invention and make the most money. It does not matter who came up with the idea first. It is the one that took action first!

I can run away from the lion first, and outrun the other runner so I don't get eaten alive; yet in life, the other runner is the old me. Learn, change, and move forward. I am not running away from the lion; I am running toward my goals and dreams. You have the power of choice. Take action now, and claim what's yours.

# Chapter 5

# Perception of Reality

**Mentality = Reality**

Many times, I've heard people say, "I'm just not a morning person," or "I am not confident enough," or they simply say, "That is not who I am." We tell ourselves who we think we are, instead of discovering who we can become. There is a quote that came to me, in 2001, when I was 22 years of age, doing business to business sales. As I gave the sales meeting, I told my fellow salesmen and saleswomen, *"Your mentality is your reality; if you can change your mentality, you can change your reality."* That is a quote that I have lived by ever since. You see, a mentally handicapped individual, or a crazy person (like some of our family members), only knows his or her reality to be what their mind tells them it is. Therefore, by changing your mind, by learning new things and educating your mind, you can see things in a new light and from a new perspective.

Later in my personal development journey, I found a video by a speaker and author, Dr. Joe Dispenza, and his quote was similar yet different, and I loved the way he put it: *"Your personality creates your personal reality, so then if you want to create a new personal reality, a new life, you are going to have to change your personality."* Most people want to create a new reality as the same personality, and it doesn't work; you literally have to become someone else. You see, we have 60,000 to 70,000 thoughts in a day, and about 90% of those thoughts are the same thoughts as the day before. How likely then are you to change your personal reality, or your life, if you keep living by the same thoughts. The same thoughts create the same results. You must change how you think, how you act, and how you feel. You must become someone else. Most people have decided who they are and are living by a set of memory responses, living subconsciously, like driving subconsciously. Things have just become habit. You must break the habits that are not working for you, and create new habits. Create a new mentality to create a new personality; that way, you can create a new personal reality. Say it with me: "I will create a new mentality, create a new personality, have a new personal reality, and have a new life."

Our perception of reality comes mostly from our five primary senses that we use to detect what is real in our physical reality, our physical universe. Yet studies show that we are multi-sensory beings. We use these senses to detect our physical universe so that we may be able to better control our environment. Yet, usually, when we try to control our environment, we tend to go into *survival of the fittest* mode, making almost everything about competition, to outdo the other guy and obtain external power. When we choose to come from our internal power, we come from a place of love, compassion, and admiration, and we go from competition to collaboration.

My perception of reality is only my point of view of the world, based on the information or knowledge I have acquired. Your point of view may be different, even though we are looking at the same thing. By collaborating, I may be able to learn something new from you that I never noticed before, and vice versa. I can show you things that you have not learned yet. In turn, we both can expand our point of view. When we are connected through our inner spiritual universe, connecting by collaborating, we are not alone; we come to understand that everything and everyone is connected. On the other hand, if we only experience the world through our external power of competition, we tend to feel lonely, always competing and not being open. By being closed-minded, we tend to close ourselves from the rest of the universe.

**The Mirror Effect**

When you are truly engaged in a conversation with someone, and in deep conversation, once you become aware of your tone of voice and body language, you will notice that you two are in sync, matching and mirroring each other. This is something we naturally do. Next time you go to a restaurant or any public place, find two people that are really engaged in their conversation, and pay attention to the body language. You will notice that they are in sync. You can take advantage of this NLP (Neuro-Linguistic Programming) technique; match or mirror someone that you would like to connect quickly with, matching their tone of voice and body language (be subtle). You will notice a shift, and the other person will say to themselves, "I feel like I know this person, and I love his or her attitude." Why? Well, that is because we usually like people that are like us, or are who we would like to become. The people you really don't like are the ones that you do not want to be like, or there is something about them that reminds you of something that you don't like about yourself, something that you are currently trying to change, or something from your past.

When I am walking around in my reality—my universe—everything I see is simply a reflection of myself, and I call this the *Mirror Effect*. It is not necessarily a reflection of an image, but a representation or projection of my point of view, values, and beliefs. Similar to an optimist, who sees a positive world around him, when I am running into frustrating people or situations all day, I analyze myself. I usually find that there's something within myself that has been frustrating me, and I am unconsciously putting it out into the universe—an energy of frustration—and that vibe is being projected onto others, and they are just deflecting it back to me.

Perception is projection. You can only perceive what is already in your conscious and unconscious mind. When you are able to be aware of what's going on in your unconscious mind, you can trace it back to the root of the issue, and either adjust or fix it.

Now, let's say that someone is being rude to you. You understand that it's just their projection. Maybe there is something that you did unconsciously to direct that negative energy toward you. Whatever the case may be, it is best to respond, not react; meaning you are going to think before you speak, and stay calm, discuss, and defuse the situation. Stay calm! I know it takes practice to not react and reflect the same negative energy at the other person with whom you are arguing. This is why, many times, an argument escalates. We are not only adding more firewood, we are adding lighter fluid to the situation. AHHHH!

Now, take a deep breath, stay calm, and respond. Remember, when emotions are high, intelligence is low, and when emotions are low, intelligence is high. Now, if you are able to stay calm, and the other person's emotions are still high, it is best to wait until they are calm, and discuss the situation at a later time. It is also wise to wait until you are calm before you make any major decision or choice.

I remember being in a bad relationship in my early twenties, and our emotions were high, and we were almost yelling at each other …Okay, we were yelling, especially if the neighbors said they could hear us. We would break up and get back together, and break up and get back together again. It was this endless cycle that went on for years. I remember when we actually ended our relationship for good, and it was when we were both calm and sitting on the back patio of my apartment, one nice cool evening. Sitting in a few moments of silence, I said calmly, "I think it's time we end the relationship for good; it's not working out." And she replied, "It's because you haven't tried!" "What?" I said. "We have both tried and tried, and we've spent X amount of years trying. Do you want to spend another X amount of years, and then come back to the same conclusion? Let's just end it here and save us both some time." She replied in a calm voice, "Okay, that's true; let's end it then." After that calm conversation, it was finally the end of that relationship.

Remember, the world you see around you is a projection of you. From now on, walk through life with your head high, with good posture, and a smile on your face. Live from cause and not from effect.

*Art C. Guerrero*

## The Illusion of Time

Have you noticed that the same people that say, "I don't have any time!" are the same people that say, "I'm just chilling," or "I'm just killing some time?" Then they wonder why they don't have time. Remember, the only way to have time is to make time. Time is an illusion. Albert Einstein taught us about the law of relativity. A minute can seem like an hour, and an hour can seem like a minute. When you are waiting for something to happen, anticipating, it seems like forever, yet time flies when you are having fun.

I've learned that it's about how we use our time or how we spend our time. We all get the same 24 hours every day, and yet we see many successful people that are able to run more than one business and still have time to spend with their loved ones.

Now, visualize a large jar, and fill it to the top with large rocks. Do you think it's full? Can we add anything else? Add some small rocks, and those rocks will fall in between the gaps of the large rocks. Once it's full of small rocks, is it full? Add some sand, and it will fill in between the rocks; and once you fill it to the top with sand, you can still add water and fill it up to the top. The rocks and pebbles symbolize tasks—your things to do. Now, just imagine if you fill up the jar, starting with the water or sand. Once it fills to the top, there is no room to fit anything else. Just like the jar, we fill up our time with small tasks that really don't have much importance. Some items we can delegate. Do you know that there are certain grocery stores where you can order online and have them delivered to your home? Do you like watching a movie? Well, every now and then it's okay, but there are some people that watch too much TV and movies every day. Listening to music is great, but every now and then, listen to a podcast or some audiobooks, on your commute. Instead of seeing a movie, read a book. Instead of just entertaining your mind all the time, educate and expand your mind. Learn something new, and complete at least one goal each day that will move you forward in life, and towards your long-term goals.

I now manage my time like I manage my money. Some say time is money. I believe time is more valuable, because you can always make money, but your time is something you'll never get back. To manage money, I write down how much I'm spending on each thing every day. Then I thought, "Hey! I will write down how much time I spend on the things I do each day. Then I will know exactly how much time I'm spending on certain items." Wow, this was incredible. I started to notice that there were some things that were taking me way too long, of which I could have just hired someone else to do them, and it would save me the time, because my time is valuable. Not only will the task be completed in less time, but it would also free me up to do the things I love: spending time with my family, learning and teaching, to name just a few.

The majority of people trade their time for money, and successful people trade their money for time. While there might be some pride in *do-it-yourself*, it's really not worth it.

I remember my dad teaching me how to do an oil-change on the car. I remember us doing it on a Saturday, and taking about an hour to do it, if not more. First, we would get dressed in some old clothes, since we might get dirty lying on the floor under the car. We had to get all the items we needed from the auto store, and then finally change the oil and oil filter. Done. Wait, where do we dispose of the used oil now? I could have just taken the car to the Quick-Lube oil-changing mechanic, who would have had it done in 10–15 minutes. And sure, I'm going to spend a little bit more money, but how much time did I save? Grant Cardone said it best: *"No one became a millionaire by SAVING MONEY; they did it by focusing on MAKING MONEY."* With that said, it's not all about *saving* time, as much as it is about *making* time. Think about it: Would you spend your money for more time? By having more time, what would you do? Do the things you love and are passionate about, because when you are doing what you love, and are making money at the same time, it's no longer work—you're getting paid to do the things you love.

## Orchestrate Importance

Instead of saying, "I don't have time," ask, "Is this a priority?" We must learn to orchestrate what's important to us, and arrange or combine tasks to achieve a desired or maximum effect in our lives. There are some tasks that we can knock out at the same time. As the saying goes, kill two birds with one stone. In our family business that my wife and I own and run, we tell our employees to always think about what else can be running in the background while they're working on a current project. Many times, there is a printer that we can have running while we are cutting paper, or have the business card cutting machine cutting cards automatically while we are working on the folding machine. There is always something that can be happening or delegated, which others can be doing for you; thus, duplicating yourself. Instead of wanting to do everything yourself, and wishing you had more time, train others to be leaders as well. It works better when you have a team of leaders around you, and you get more work done.

Knowing what's important to you, and how to prioritize, will have the most impact in achieving your goals. Knowing your intentions and your goals will give you a better angle on your point of view, when you know what you're aiming at. *"If you aim at nothing, you will hit it every time,"* as Zig Ziglar said. Write down your goals, and don't worry about how it's going to happen or how you are going to achieve them. Just be outrageous with your dreams and goals. Anything is possible. For me, I have found that it's better to see the end result, visualizing myself at the finish line, and all of my supporters, family, and friends cheering me on. Then I can begin to reverse engineer how I got there. The more times that I visualize and meditate on my goals, the clearer I get on what steps I need to take, and the more opportunities will present themselves. As I take action and take the steps necessary, my goals begin to manifest.

As you take action moving forward, not only will people see how committed you are, what will also happen is that the Universe and/or God will start assisting and giving you more opportunities to choose from. When you know your end goal, you will choose the opportunity and path that is better aligned with the goals: the path that will get you there, not just faster but with the knowledge and skills that will better equip you to get to the finish line, or at least to the next checkpoint. Many times, when you get to the finish line, you create another goal and advance to the next level. The game of success is never really over. Remember, it's a journey, so keep moving forward.

## The Illusion of Fear

There are many people who say that FEAR is an acronym for False Evidence Appearing Real. Now, what does that mean? When danger is present, we may get scared of what we *think* might happen; yet we are trying to predict something that has not happened, and we usually believe that it might result in a negative outcome. The truth is that the future outcome is only one of many possibilities. We usually fear things that we do not understand. Therefore, the more we are able to read a situation, and learn and predict the outcome, the less we will fear. But there are some situations that will just happen, and we will not understand, and it will catch us by surprise. Therefore, let's really define what we are feeling. I believe that FEAR has another acronym: **F**eeling **E**xcited **A**nd **R**eady!

If there is something that we are not understanding, it is an *unknown*, and as we learned in Chapter three, there are wonders in the unknown—it's something new. Let's get excited, because we are about to learn something new and expand our minds, our horizons, and our universe. Even with danger, we are about to learn a new way to overcome a new obstacle.

I've learned to view fear like having Spiderman's *Spidy senses*. All your body is doing is putting you in a state of awareness, ready and alert to be able to take on the new challenge. We get this **F**eeling of

**E**xcitement **A**nd we get **R**eady.

Whatever comes your way, be ready to overcome; you are a warrior. There is no reason to fear failure, because there is no failure, just feedback. You learn a new way not to do it, and figure out another way to go about it; keep being persistent until you become successful.

If we look at the definition of fear in the dictionary, it means an unpleasant emotion caused by the BELIEF that someone or something is dangerous, likely to cause pain, or is a threat. Notice it says *by the belief*, which is something that we are creating in our mind by assuming. When you ASSUME, you only make an ASS out of U and ME.

Every emotion is bringing you back to *love*. The bible says that God is love, and therefore, true love is Godly, and love is spiritual, which is why we all want it. We are able to manifest our physical universe when we are connected to our spiritual universe, to love, and to God. There is a scripture that says, *"If God is with us, then who can be against us?"* Which makes sense when people say, "Love conquers all," because God is love. With love, we are able to come from a place of admiration, which overcomes fear, sadness, loneliness, anger, frustration, and all those other negative feelings. When you are coming from a place of love and admiration, you are dwelling in a spiritual realm, and you are able to align your mind, body, and soul.

Fear is a catalyst for inaction. We tend to live in the past, with regret or fear of the future, instead of living in the NOW. If we flip the word, NOW, around, it spells WON. This is where we can win in life. Fear usually has us living in the future, in a negative way, asking, "What if this goes wrong; or what if it goes right? Am I ready?" Don't worry about HOW; just know that you will succeed. HOW is not important. What is important is that you live in the NOW, and radiate from LOVE and ADMIRATION.

## Observation & Awareness

The key is to observe and be aware of what's happening, not just around you in your external world, but more importantly, what is happening internally. What does your mind interpret, and what are the emotions you are having? And what does this mean? A friend once asked me why it is that we feel pain. Let's suppose that you are preparing a meal, and you are cutting some vegetables, and you accidently nick your finger, making a slight incision. You yell "ouch" and pull away, right? Pain is your body's way of keeping you safe. If you kept cutting, you might end up cutting your finger completely off. In this same way, the Universe wants to keep you safe, and will alert you when danger is present. Have the awareness to know when something does not feel right and is causing you pain. How many times have you been a situation, whether it's a relationship, a job, a business deal, or any situation that you knew did not feel right, and in the end, you ended up paying the consequences? That relationship or friendship kept causing you pain and stress, but you kept telling yourself that it would get better, instead of listening to your heart and your emotions. What is your gut instinct telling you? What is the Universe telling you? There are some people that ignore these signs, and they end up living a very unhappy life, full of stress. Observe, and be aware of your unconscious mind as well.

I was once talking with a speaker and teacher, who spent time with monks. He said that we live in an age of constant chatter; there is noise everywhere. Not only is media and social media trying to keep your attention all the time, we always have to have some video or audio playing in the background. It is important to quiet everything down, and sit in silence: slowing the breathing down, and slowing the mind from doing all that thinking—the mind chatter. Deep breathing will center you and bring you into the present, and into the moment of NOW. Here is where you can finally listen to your body and your soul.

As you observe, it is also important to expand your awareness. Sometimes you get stuck in tunnel vision mode, where you get caught up in one thing and all the details about it. You miss the bigger picture. What else is going on? Step back and look at things from a different angle. Expand your awareness. By practicing this every day, you will be able to overcome challenges with more ease, and you will notice more options available to you. The Hawaiians practice *Hakalau*. It is a meditative trance, or a joyful awareness, which is used to observe and interpret the world around them. Widening one's field of vision, and entering this state of trance, is a process of entering a field of expanded consciousness. Hakalau is one of the reasons a shaman will seldom look at his apprentice. Hakalau is extremely useful for athletes, dancers, musicians, and artists. Many creative people use some kind of expanded awareness to go unconscious at times.

Look forward and pick a spot in front of you, about 25 degrees above eye level. Now, relax your vision, to get out of the tunnel vision. Begin to expand your attention and awareness into your peripheral vision; observe and be aware of everything, including sounds and feelings. As you observe your feelings as well, you will become aware of not only your exterior physical universe, but you will also have more awareness of your inner self.

When you are able to tap into your unconscious mind, you will be closer to the source of your creativity and your spirituality. Children, from the ages of zero to seven, mostly operate from their unconscious mind. Do you notice how creative and how happy they are? It is when we develop our conscious mind that we start to make life harder than what it really is. Let's be more aware of our internal and external selves, expanding our awareness. Many times, the answer is closer than we know it to be, or has already been answered. When we operate from our unconscious, we are happier and more creative, and we have the awareness to navigate life with more ease.

# Chapter 6

# Exchanging Ideas

**Sell to Propel**

Launch your life toward your goals. Selling is vital for your success in business and in your personal life. When I'm talking about selling, I'm not just talking about a product or service; I'm talking about ideas. You see, we are all salesmen and saleswomen. We are selling ideas every day, and we are being sold ideas as well. If you are not the one doing the selling, then you are being sold to. In other words, if you are not making money, then you are spending money. When you are working on your business, or at your place of business, you are making money, getting paid from your customers, and/or getting a paycheck. Usually, when you're not at work or working on your business, you're spending money—clothes, movies, dinners, entertainment, etc. You are selling or being sold to. Okay, now that we are seeing this from that point of view, and while spending money is not a bad thing, it's just that we tend to spend more than what we are making. Success in business, and in your personal life, means that you need to do more selling of ideas than you are buying; and not just any ideas, but great and positive ideas. In the past, we have bought into other people's ideas: "Aw, that's too hard; you won't ever achieve that. You don't have what it takes; what if you fail?" Yet most of those ideas are ideas that those people bought into themselves, and now they are trying to sell you on those ideas. Think about it: How many times has someone purchased a movie ticket, and after they saw the movie, told you all about that movie, and that you should go see it. They want to reaffirm to themselves that they made a good decision, and are now selling you on the idea that it's a good movie.

One of the most important sales you can ever make is to *sell yourself*. Most people, who have been in sales, understand this: getting your customer to like you, and selling them on the idea that you are similar and have similar interests. Once the customer likes you, it will be easier to make the sale. Now, if you are doing this, and are genuinely listening to the customer and are attentive to his or her needs, and you are able to gain rapport, then this will work. What I am also talking about, in regard to selling yourself, is when you, yourself, buy into your own ideas. You must believe in the product, service, and idea, to the point that you have bought into them.

One night at a restaurant, a waitress asked my wife and me, "How do you get your daughter to eat her vegetables?" Then, right when she finished asking us, our daughter, G.G., said, "I love broccoli." We just smiled, and I asked the waitress, "Let me ask you one question. Do you eat vegetables?" She answered, "No." There you have it: How does anyone expect their child to eat vegetables, when they, themselves, haven't bought into the idea that vegetables are good for them, and they aren't leading by example? Just as it is with kids—monkey see, monkey do—adults also have to see that you have also bought into the same ideas.

Be careful of what ideas you are selling. Most of the time, you don't even realize that you are selling. When you are *telling* someone about something or someone, you are actually selling. You must remind yourself, "When I'm *telling*, I'm *selling*." For example, I'm excited when I am telling you that I just bought a Range Rover, and how much my wife and I love the vehicle; and I'm telling you about all the features and how smooth the ride is, and we believe we made a great investment. With all the excitement, and telling you truthfully from the heart as I TELL you about the vehicle, I indirectly SELL you on the vehicle (unconsciously). Now, next time you are thinking about buying a vehicle, you might consider the vehicle I TOLD *(SOLD)* you about. Remember what you are telling people, and more importantly, what you are telling yourself about yourself. What ideas are you taking on about who you are and what you are capable of? How much energy is going on behind the story you tell yourself, and how much excitement; and how confident are you about your ideas and your reality?

**The People Business**

What business are you in? I used to think that I was in the printing business, and at one point in my life, I was in the tattoo business and the DJ business. Then I realized that no matter what I was doing, the truth was that I was in the *people business*. It's not about selling a product or service as much as it is about meeting the needs of people. How can I help them; will my product or service really meet their needs?

*Art C. Guerrero*

Most customers end up NOT buying, and walking away from a purchase because they believe that the idea, product, or service will NOT meet their needs. Many times, there's not enough information to convince them otherwise. I know this, seeing it from the customer's point of view. I went to a seminar and was being sold a product, and I was not really convinced. I told the salesman that I was not going to buy, and that I was not sure at this present time if this was for me. He asked me what it was about the product. I didn't give too much information; I just said that it was too much at this time. The salesman proceeded to tell me that it's never about the money; it's about the product. While I felt he was a bit pushy, I started to really ask myself the same questions. While I did believe that the product was too much, I had the money, but it was more because I felt it was too much for that particular product. In other words, I didn't believe I was getting enough value for myself for that particular product. *It's never about the money?* Okay, yeah, I guess I was starting to see how he believed that. Then he offered another product that was five times more, and I sat down with the sales guy and the speaker himself. The transformational speaker asked me if I believed and was confident that he could help me. He looked at me confidently and spoke from the heart, and genuinely said, "I will do everything possible, and I know I can help you succeed."

I told him that while I did see the value and how this product fits my needs, I also made an agreement with my wife that I would not purchase anything at this seminar; and to keep my wife's confidence in me, I needed to keep my agreements. The speaker agreed and said, "Okay, we are not going to sell you anything at this event," and he told his staff that I was not allowed to buy anything at this event. This showed me that he was considerate of me and my needs. He was more concerned about meeting my needs than selling me the product. Throughout the rest of the event, I was upgraded to VIP seating, and was genuinely being taken care of and shown that they wanted me to be part of their family, if you will.

Later that week, I talked it over with my wife, and we purchased the product that was five times more than the original product, because that was more fitting to what I was looking for. What really sold me was their customer service; they are in the people business, and are willing to go above and beyond for their people. A couple days later, we ended up purchasing the product, and we also received a gift basket from them. WOW! They were going the extra mile for their people. When we are in the people business, this does not only apply to customers; it applies to everyone. We need to be listening to the other person's needs. The more people you help, the more money you make. I also believe that the more you help people reach their goals, the more people are willing to help you reach your goals. It is the law of reciprocity. When I say it applies to everyone, I mean everyone.

We want our kids to listen to us, yet are we listening to them and what they want? Once, I was talking to a six-year-old, and then an adult asked me why I was talking to the kid like an adult. I replied, "I'm talking to him like a person." Most people just boss kids around, without actually having a conversation with them. Maybe the kid doesn't understand what he or she is being asked. After all, they are just small people who are learning how the world works. Let's take the time to teach them. Just like some adults and some customers, we must listen to their objections and questions, and educate them;

and then they will be motivated to take action. Remember, you are not in the "X" business, you are in the *people business*. This is one major contributing factor in what has made me successful in our printing business. We are more concerned about our customers and meeting their needs than just providing a product. With us, at WTBS Printing, we want you to have a great *experience* in doing business with us.

I had a customer tell me one day, "I'm going to be honest with you, Art; I have shopped around, and you guys are a little bit higher in price than everyone else in town, but the reason I love doing business with you guys is your awesome customer service, and you take the time to listen to the customer. You sit down and go over everything, making sure it is exactly the way we want it. On top of all that, you guys are super-fast; you get the job done when you say it will be done. I am confident the product will be done right and on time. Overall, it's a great experience here at WTBS Printing." You see, it was not about the money. With this customer, we met his needs, which was more important to him than how much it cost. He saw the value.

**The Power of Agreements**

Do you want to get your way in life more? Would you like to make more money? Keeping your agreements is very important. Your word should be law. Whatever you say, you are going to do; DO IT!

Do you really understand how powerful words are? Words are your bond. Even the Bible, the word of God, is a bond, and not even

God can change it. Whatever God says, is. That is how powerful words are.

My mentor and millionaire friend, Raymond Aaron, asked me once, "Do you know why successful people get their way more, in life and in wealth? Because they keep their agreements and are backed by confidence." He said, "Poor people make too many agreements, and most of those agreements were made just because they were wanting to be nice. Then they don't keep their agreements. We must learn to make fewer agreements, and only make agreements that we can keep." He then asked, "Do you want more money?" I smiled as I thought: *Well, doesn't everyone?* I replied, "Yes." Then he asked me, "Do you know what money is?" Puzzled by this question, I was trying to figure out what he meant. Raymond then asked me, "How can you get more money if you don't even know what it really is?" Wow, okay. I just looked at him and waited for him to proceed to tell me. He said, "Money is agreements backed by confidence." We keep our agreements, and by doing so, we build other's confidence in us.

I started to think about my life and when I was struggling and just living paycheck to paycheck. I realized that this was very true in my life: I would make agreements and not keep them. I would tell someone that I would do something or be somewhere, or that I would help them out with something, but I would not follow through. I used to have a lot of excuses. I was not reliable or dependable, but once I started to keep my word, and keep my promises, I started to build confidence in others and myself. I also came to understand that in order for me to keep my promises, I had to make fewer promises, which meant I had to learn when to say no. If I knew I was not able to keep that promise and follow through, I had to be honest with myself and others, and just tell them, "No." People ask, "Why is it so hard to trust?" I ask, "Why is it so hard to keep a promise?" Write down your agreements, and keep your promises. Just as you can make commitments, you must also learn when to de-commit. At the first sight of knowing that you will not be able to keep that agreement, be straight up and honest, and let that person or group know at the first appropriate time. This might happen, so do your best to not make the commitment or agreement unless you are certain you can keep it. If you are not sure if you can, then communicate it and let them know you will agree as soon as you know for sure you can keep that promise. Be open and honest with yourself and others, and keep agreements with others and yourself.

I have definitely noticed how my business has grown, by keeping my agreements. A customer told us that someone told them, "When Art and Yeya, at WTBS Printing, say they will have the order ready on a certain date, they always have it ready." This was *word of mouth* that we keep our word. I am even more confident in myself, because I keep my own agreements—my own promises to myself.

## 100% Attitude – Smile

Having a great attitude is very important in everything you do, in business and in your personal life. Smiles are contagious. Have you ever noticed, when you smile at a newborn baby, they smile back at you? They don't even know what you are saying, or anything about the world; they just arrived, yet they smile back at you. Babies feel the positive energy you send them by smiling. This is done on a unconscious level, and kids operate more from their unconscious mind, since they are still developing the conscious mind (their critical thinking mind.) They tend to mimic as a way of learning—matching and mirroring. When we smile at someone—I mean really smile at them, with a big genuine smile—they feel that energy, and they will smile back at you, and they will send you that same burst of positive energy. When I look at someone all serious, they look back at me all serious, and I start wondering why they are looking at me all serious. They receive that energy and transmission through that frequency, and reflect it back to me, saying the same thing, "Why is he looking at me all serious?" *(the mirror effect)*

In order to have a great attitude all the time, you must protect your attitude. We are all human, and there are things that will unfortunately happen. The question is, how will you respond, and how long will you stay in that feeling? Analyze what happened and why, and what the lesson is. What can you learn from this? Then, work back to having a great attitude.

Everything is 100% energy, which is why everything is 100% attitude. The attitude that you are having is producing energy at a certain frequency. Similar to radio waves, if you are tuned into a certain frequency, you will attract everything on that channel, on that frequency. If things in life are not happening the way that I want them to, I take a step back and check my attitude: What energy am I giving off? I take a few moments to quiet myself and be still. Then I take a few deep breaths, usually for about a minute. This tends to get me out of my head and back into my body, and to center myself in the

NOW. Once centered, I start to smile and begin feeling joy and happiness. If need be, I'll think of something or someone—my wife, my daughter, a memory— that leads me back to having a great attitude.

Back in 2002, when I was 23 years old, I was a door-to-door salesman, but more of a business-to-business peddler. I was a top salesman and was running sales meetings three times a week. One particular day after work, I went home, where I lived with my brother and a few other fellow salesmen who were also my roommates. When we entered the home, we were all shocked to find out that our home had been robbed. Missing were seven of my oil paintings that I had personally painted, along with TVs, a Sony PlayStation, and many other things. In my room, on the wall, spray painted in big orange letters, were the words, "FUCK YOU." Wow, what happened? The rest of the night, we all just kept going through the house, looking to see what all was missing. Exhausted, I just said, "Oh well, there's nothing we can do about it now. I need to get some rest; I have to work tomorrow."

The next morning, I woke everyone up to get ready to go to work, but many of them were not really wanting to. I told them, "There is nothing we can do about it now; let's get out of this funk and go make some money!" We all got paid on commission, so if we didn't work, we didn't get paid. That morning was my turn to run the meeting. The owner asked me if I was up to it. I replied, "Hell, yeah!" I got up in front of the room, in front of thirty-five salesmen, and told them, with a smile on my face, "Guess what happened to me and my roommates last night?!" They all replied simultaneously, "WHAT HAPPENED!?" I said, with a big smile, "Aw, man, it was crazy! We got robbed last night!"

Still smiling, while chuckling a little, I said, "But you know what?" They replied simultaneously again, "WHAT!?" I answered in a sarcastic voice, "Some people would not even have come to work, because they would have been too upset and sad, and having a pity party, saying that they don't feel like working today. But my roommates, my brother Sway, and I still came to work! And even though they took TVs, my oil paintings, and many other things, DO YOU KNOW WHAT IS THE ONE THING THEY DID NOT TAKE? ...THE ONE THING THEY CAN NEVER TAKE FROM ME?" They eagerly replied again, "WHAT!?" I responded proudly, smiling, with a loud voice, "THEY CAN NEVER TAKE **MY ATTITUDE!**" Everyone cheered and was going crazy! I was still smiling, and I told them, "Today, I'm going to outsell everyone, because now there is more room at home for me to buy some NEW STUFF!" "Remember guys, the one thing that nobody can ever take from you is your attitude! If someone takes it, it's because you were not protecting it, and you allowed them to take it. Now, let's go have some FUN and make some money!"

I went out that day and had one of my best sales days ever. I always remembered that day, and constantly remind myself, "The one thing that no one can ever take from me, is my attitude!" Whatever you do in life, business or personal, remember to smile, always have a great attitude, and above all, have fun! If you are not having fun, what is the point?

*Art C. Guerrero*

## The Power of NO!

While some people don't like hearing the word, *no*, or being told, *no*, for that matter, I believe it's only because they have a different meaning of the word. Everything is perspective; therefore, let's look at the word, *no*, from a different angle. If we flip it around and spell it backwards, it becomes, *on*. When I hear the word, *no*, I see it as a switch being flipped to *on*. I get fired up—it's GO time, baby!

In sales, we were taught about the *Law of Averages*, meaning you will usually only sell to 10% of the people you talk to; therefore, you will get about 90% *no's*, all day. Now, the percentage can fluctuate as you get better at the psychology of the sale; none the less, you will usually get more no's than yes's. Therefore, we must get the no's out of the way; it's part of the process, to get closer to the yes's. The faster we get the no's out of the way, the faster we get to the yes's. Along the way, we start to understand that if we are getting too many *no's*, then there is probably something we don't *KNOW*. What can we learn about why we got that *no*? Is there something we could have done differently? At the same time, there are just some people that will say no; and it could very well mean *no* right now, and that it's just not the right time. Don't take the "no" personally. They are not saying no to you directly; they are saying no to the product, service, or idea, which just doesn't fit their need. They are definitely not saying no to you.

One day, while working in San Jose, California, after being promoted to National Sales Trainer, I was training a new sales associate. We were out doing some sales, and on our way back to the car to get more merchandise, I approached a young lady and began to talk to her. "How are you doing on this lovely day?" I said, with a smile on my face, and with a great attitude. She replied, "Wonderful." I started to tell her about how we were out doing a promotion, and wanted her opinion on a product. I placed the product in her hand and told her how we were letting them go today for the wholesale price, at 75% off, and asked her, "Is that fair?" She looked at me and quickly said, "I'm not buying; no thank you."

I smiled and told her that I was just asking if it was fair, and not if she wanted to buy one. I just smiled, looked at her with confidence, and asked her, "Hey, look, let's forget about that; I think you are very beautiful, and you seem like an awesome person to hang out with. Do you think I could get your phone number?" She smiled back at me, and said, "Yes, let me get a pen." I handed her a pen, and she continued smiling as she wrote her phone number down. My trainee was just observing in awe. She said, "Call me," and then she got in her car and drove off. I looked at my trainee and asked him if he wanted the number. He said, "No, aren't you going to call her?" I just crumpled up the paper and threw it away. I told him, "I wanted to show you that when she said no, she was not saying no to me; she was saying no to the product. Don't take the "no" personally. As you can see, she said no to the product, but she said yes to me." I just smiled, and my trainee just laughed and said, "Art, you're crazy."

What does *no* mean to you? The word, *no*, has great power, especially when *you* get to say it. How many times have we said yes to someone because we didn't want to disappoint them or make them feel bad—saying yes to the wrong things—bad relationships, time-consuming projects, or just taking on too many tasks? I had to learn when to say no. Having clarity on what lines up with my dreams and goals, and when I have things written down on my schedule, helps me to know if it is something I can say yes or no to. You have the power to say *no* to things that don't feel right to you, or are hurting you, or to people that are draining your energy. When you can say no to the things and people that do not align with you, then you will be able to say a true *yes,* with more conviction. The doors of opportunity will open for you. Others will see that you don't just say *yes* to anything, and that you know who you are, and that says a lot about your character. Say this with me: "When I say no, it means NO, and when I say yes, it means YES!"

## Persistence

When you are not getting the desired outcome, you keep pushing forward. As I mentioned in Chapter three, do something different to get a different result. If we do the same thing over and over again, we will more than likely get the same result.

Persistence means to have a firm or obstinate continuance in a course of action, in spite of difficulty or opposition.

Bill Bradly quoted, *"Ambition is the path to success; persistence is the vehicle you arrive in."* Many have the ambition to dream, and have goals and want to accomplish them. We make the attempt, and when we fail, we tend to just settle and say, "Well, I tried."

The word, *try*, is a word that I have eliminated from my vocabulary, because the word, *try*, just means to make an *attempt* or *effort* to do something. To me, there is no *try*; either I will do it or not do it. Don't try; just do it. Don't settle for mediocre, or for something that is just okay. When someone asks you how you are doing, don't say fine, or good; you want to be able to answer with a true, heartfelt, *"I'm doing GREAT!"* Or, *awesome, fantastic, and spectacular!* There is greatness inside you. Persist and keep going; it's not over until you succeed! Kids are the best at it: When they want something really bad, they will do anything to get it, and they will keep asking you for it, until they succeed. As adults, we don't have to nag. We are not pushy; we are just persistent. Have a great attitude, be patient, and stay persistent.

The one thing you do not want to have is regret. When you get old, and you're lying on your death bed, you don't want to be wishing you had accomplished your goals, traveled more, or done more.

Some of us have a subconscious program in our minds, a voice that is telling us, "You are not good enough and will not succeed. Look at your family; no one else has made it. They all have sugar diabetes; why will you be any different?" Yet it is not that diabetes RUNS in the family, it's that nobody in the family RUNS. If we are doing the same thing as our family—eating the same way, having the same beliefs—we will have the same result. It starts with being consciously aware of our unconscious, and being aware of our way of thinking, our beliefs, and values, so that we begin to change.

Thomas Edison quoted, *"I have not failed. I just found 10,000 ways that won't work."* When we are able to continue to remind ourselves that we will succeed no matter what, and that failure is just a stepping stone, we will be able to change our unconscious habits, where we can start to have unconscious success. We will have an automatic response to how we look at our obstacles. Eliminate the *problem*. From now on, we just have challenges and obstacles, which we will overcome through persistence, because it is not over until we succeed.

# Chapter 7

# Reinvent Your Mind

**Discover Your Path**

Many want to be their own boss and to own a business, yet they are not sure of what they want to do. They get into a business because they know how to do the business, not necessarily because they love the business. In just the same way, others live their personal lives just going through the motions: working a job, providing for the family, spending time with the kids, eating, sleeping, waking up, and doing it all over again. Because that is what you are supposed to do. While these things are important, we must have passion in our lives. We sometimes live mundane lives, because we have no love for what we do, and we have no purpose.

I remember a time when I found myself going through the motions, and I would ask myself, "Is this it? There has to be more than this." Usually, when I felt this way, I felt like there was something missing. What I noticed was that I was going in circles—going through the motions, the same routines—and it all felt too familiar. There was nothing new. When that happens, well... to be honest, it gets a bit boring. There has to be excitement in our lives! We have to have fun! I always say, "If you are not having fun, then what's the point?"

How do you find your path? This is a very important question, and a question that I continue to ask myself from time to time. "If money was not an obstacle, what would you do?" "If all your finances were taken care of, what would you do?" Hmmmmm? Now, that's a great question. What do you have a passion for? What would you love to do—paint all day, travel around the world—what? Well, let me tell you: I guarantee you that even though you may think you could not make a living by doing your hobby or passion, there is a way that you can do that, and make money at it, and possibly get rich by doing it. There are no limits. The only limits we have are the ones we put in front of ourselves.

There is a scene from the movie, *Fight Club*, which I always remembered: when Tyler Durden, Brad Pitt's character, grabs the clerk from the convenience store and takes him to the back of the store, at gun point. Then he asks the clerk to give him his wallet. Tyler then reads his driver's license, and says, "Raymond K. Hessel, you are going to die." Then Tyler notices an expired community college I.D., and he asks him, "What did you want to be?" Raymond is shaking and whimpering... he's so scared that he doesn't answer. Tyler asks him again, with a more aggressive tone, "What did you want to be, Raymond K. Hessel?" There was still no answer, and Tyler pulls the hammer back on the gun. *Click*..."The question, Raymond! What did you want to be?!" Raymond finally replies, "Veterinarian; animals and stuff." Tyler says, "That means you would have to get more schooling?" Raymond replies, "Too much schooling," and Tyler replies, "Would you rather be dead? Would you rather die, here on your knees, in the back of a convenience store?" Raymond answers with a whimper, "No, please."

## The Art of Unconscious Success

Then Tyler takes out Raymond's driver's license from the wallet, and tells him, "I'm keeping your license. I know where you live. If you are not on your way to becoming a veterinarian in six weeks, you will be dead. Now run on home." Tyler's friend (Edward Norton's character), watching the whole thing, asks Tyler, "What was the point of that?" Tyler replies, "Tomorrow will be the most beautiful day of Raymond K. Hessel's life. His breakfast will taste better than any meal you and I have ever tasted." Wow! Yeah, that made sense. Now that the Raymond character had purpose in his life, and he would be doing what he loves, everything else around him would brighten up. This is true. I've noticed that my days are much brighter, and it really seems as if all the colors are more vivid. It's a joy that overcomes and fills my life. Meals do taste better. When we resonate on a high energy level— a joyous frequency—we attract things on the similar frequency.

What will it take for you to get back on track to doing what you love, and what you were meant to do? Don't wait for something extreme to really knock you down and have a gun to your head before you react. Don't be like me. Life had to really hit me hard upside my head, when I hit the pavement, falling off the motorcycle, going 90 mph. If you feel you are just surviving, and you've lost the spark of life, then notice the signs and the symptoms that something is not right; if you don't do something about it, then your condition may worsen, and your life may need severe resuscitation to bring you back to life. In doing what you love, you will not only feel alive; you will truly thrive, just like a tree that thrives and bears beautiful delicious fruit. It's not so much about discovering your path, but about re-discovering.

## The Transformation

Preparation is important before one goes through a dramatic change, reconstruction, or metamorphosis. We must prepare for our transformation. Similarly, a caterpillar will eat enough to have plenty of energy to construct its protective casing, its cocoon; then it will begin its journey to evolve and transform. The first process for the caterpillar is to begin to digest itself, releasing enzymes to dissolve all of its tissue.

For us humans, once our eyes and minds are open—once we have clarity of our goals, and we know what we want to become, and once we commit to change and to transform—we can begin to dissolve our old selves, our previous beliefs and values that no longer serve us. We can begin to construct our new personality, our new life, our new way of thinking and feeling, just as caterpillars have certain highly organized groups of cells that survive the digestive process. These cells are known as imaginal disc that remain dormant until the caterpillar is ready for metamorphosis.

We, too, have greatness inside us. Once we dissolve and strip away all that we have accumulated along the way, we can begin to notice our true selves—peeling away the layers, the titles, the ego. We can shine through our hearts with our pure greatness, pushing with all our might to expand our energy throughout our body and our Universe. This is a process, similar to the caterpillar evolving into a butterfly, and we must do it by ourselves. If you were to help a butterfly out of its cocoon as it was pushing through to emerge, it would not finish its process to push all of its fluid and protein into its wings, and the butterfly would not survive. In this same way, we must push ourselves to evolve and transform. We prepare with the information we receive, from books, teachers, speakers, and seminars, as we educate ourselves. It is our teachers and knowledge that show us the way. We can lead a horse to water, but we cannot make him drink. We can be shown the door, yet we have to walk through it. We can have the information that will change our lives, yet we must apply ourselves and take action.

It is that struggle that fortifies us. Just as gold or silver must pass through the fire in order to be molded into a beautiful chalice or cup, we too must pass through a similar process. Now, if you have not encountered a life changing event that drives you and pushes you toward a better you, then imagine what will happen if you don't change, if you keep going down this path—where will it lead you? What is the worst possible reality?  Dwell in that existence for a moment—what do you see, hear, and feel? Is that so intolerable that it forces you to begin your quest for personal transformation? Only you will know when you have had enough and are ready to transform.

**Creativity with Passion**

Albert Einstein said, *"Imagination is more important that knowledge."* I believe he said this because, without using our imagination, we would not know what to do with the knowledge. Imagination allows us to be creative and to imagine the many possibilities.

*Art C. Guerrero*

We are all artists. If you look around at everything—for example, it took an artist to create the chair, the table, the building, your car—everything is designed and created by an artist. I remember that even Subway Sandwiches call themselves *the sandwich artist*. Being an artist is not necessarily painting or drawing a picture. We are all artists; we all have a skill or a talent. You have greatness inside you; there is something that you are passionate about. The ability to be creative is what makes you an artist.

We are all creative, it's just that some express it in different areas, not always having to do with fine arts. Some individuals may have just not practiced being creative enough. Some people stop being creative, because somewhere down the line, someone told them, "That is not good enough. What's that? That's not art." You listened to someone that was not even an art major or art professor—someone that knows nothing about art. In the same way, we have listened to other's advice about money, even if they were not doing great in their finances. Where are you getting your mentoring, coaching, and advice from? Well, take it from me, as an artist in all areas of fine arts, to majoring in graphic design, everyone not only has the potential, but is an artist at heart. Think of a time when you were a child and you loved to color, play with clay, build with Lego, etc. You were having fun being creative, being passionate as an artist.

Every business requires the creative mind of an artist, to think outside the box. The logic, mechanics, and technical things in business keep the business running, yet it is creative thinking that inspires growth—having the imagination to create more opportunities. In our personal lives, the logic and mechanics build habits, yet it is our creative side that gets us out of the routine and reminds us to have fun, and to do something different and exciting.

I believe that you can now agree with me that you are an artist in some way, form, or fashion. You are creative, and you can continue to develop your creativity more and more each day. Do something you love, find inspiration, unplug (or just do nothing), be willing to take risk, and reward your curiosity. Curiosity will lead you to creativity. Make time for creativity! Being more creative will allow you to look at things from different angles, and to overcome challenges, which will allow you to build your confidence as well, and be more resourceful in business and in your personal life. Imagination is very important in all aspects of life. You are an artist; create your life with passion.

*"The best way to predict your future is to create it."*
— Abraham Lincoln

*"The world is my canvas; my mind is the paint brush."*
— Art C. Guerrero

## Introspection

Introspection means observation or examination of one's own mental and emotional state, mental processes, etc.: the act of looking within oneself.

One way that I do this every day is by meditation. Now, I want you to understand that there are different types of meditation. The style of meditation that I particularly like to use is visualization meditation. This is an amazing way to create and attract your future. The way that I do this is by finding a nice quiet place. I tend to find that the early morning and late evening is the best time to meditate. If you have difficulty finding a quiet place, as I sometimes do, use some ear plugs or earmuffs. But before I go into detail explaining my meditation style, I want to discuss how most people live their lives. Most wake up in the morning, think about their problems, and anchor themselves into certain emotions that reaffirm their personality. They remind themselves who they are, by a record of the past. Now, if thoughts are the language of the mind, and feelings are the language of the body, then most people are experiencing life neurologically, and feeling through emotions—they are experiencing a past-present reality.

When you can create a future reality, you will make new connections neurologically. Nerve cells that fire together, wire together. As you can continue to re-create your future reality, your mind and body will begin to prepare itself for this new experience, and rewire, as it now lives in this present-future reality. You unconscious mind does not know if your experience is happening in the present or is recalling a memory, or if it's a vision of the future. The unconscious mind has no concept of time. Similar to the experiment with athletes that scientists performed, they discovered that the same nerve cells in the mind and body fired together when the athlete was actually running, and when the athlete was sitting in a chair, just thinking about running.

Now, sit up straight, take a deep breath, and find your center. Relax your body and mind. Now visualize about three years into the future.

Really begin the get creative and design the future of your choice. Who are you? Where are you? What are you doing in this life event? What are you wearing? Begin to visualize the details; what do you see? Now begin to notice what sounds you hear—voices, music, all the sound effects. Now notice your kinesthetic awareness. What do you feel, internally and externally? If you are sitting in a chair, what does the material feel like; what is the temperature in the air? Are there any aromas that you smell? Is there anything that you can taste? Be aware of all of your senses in this future reality. Really soak in this possible reality. Do not concern yourself with how you got here; just know that you are here, you made it, and you're full of joy and excitement, knowing you've reached your goals and dreams. Once you have absorbed what three years from now looks like, visualize what two years from now looks like, utilizing all your senses. Observe what this looks, sounds, and feels like. Once you have visualized all the details, visualize two years from now. What has to happen, and what steps are you going to take in that year, for this to happen for you? You are reverse engineering your future reality. Where do you need to be six months from now, three months, one month? Keep visualizing each time frame with all the details, and take your time in doing so. Where are you 30 days from now, 15 days from now? Now, what has to happen one week from now? What are the steps and goals that will get you on the path to your new, amazing future reality? What are two goals, or two steps that you will take each day? At least have one major goal that you will complete each day.

In practicing your visualizations each day, your unconscious mind and body will begin to rewire itself, and the Universe will align itself with your request. The more you practice, the more the Universe and your unconscious will know your commitment. You will emit a frequency that will attract those things and people into your life. More opportunities will present themselves to you.

(Visit ucsuccess.com to download your free copy of *U.C. Success Meditation* audio file.)

## Absorb Knowledge, Evolve and Succeed

There are many things that have allowed and continue allowing me to succeed. One thing in particular that has been very crucial in obtaining success, is books. Have you ever noticed that every millionaire and successful entrepreneur has a library in their home? This is no coincidence. The reason that these millionaires and very successful individuals have obtained success, and continue to have success, is due to the fact that they are always reading books. Now, I know that there are some of you that may not be too fond of reading. Well, to be honest, neither was I, at first, which is why those that have known me since I was a teenager, are surprised that I have read so many books in recent years. If you want to be successful, and you are hungry for change, you will read more books.

I found a way that has allowed me to absorb more knowledge through books, and that is by listening to audiobooks. This is a great way to absorb many books. Make time to read, and with audiobooks, listen to them on a long drive or while on an airplane, even while waiting in a waiting room, standing in a long line, or while painting. There are many great times to knock out a book, instead of just surfing on your Facebook newsfeed, or any social media for that matter. While Facebook, Instagram, and Twitter are great tools to promote your business, or to just be social, the question is, how much time are you spending on it, and are you being productive? What are you doing each day that gets you closer to your goals?

Books and audiobooks are a great way to absorb knowledge. Attending personal growth, self-development, and transformational seminars have also allowed me to not only obtain more knowledge, but have allowed me to connect with like-minded individuals that are also on the path to evolve and achieve their goals. We are also able to hold each other accountable to insure we stay on our path, by supporting each other.

Knowledge is power! *"Imagination is more important than knowledge,"* as Albert Einstein quoted. This means that imagination is very powerful. How do you get creative with the knowledge that you gain? Part of this means that it's not just about reading books or going to seminars; it's about applying the knowledge. By applying yourself and taking action, you will begin to evolve, expanding your mind and receiving more clarity. You will begin to connect the dots. You will understand yourself and your purpose. Having new knowledge will give you new tools to assist you on your journey to success. Your imagination and creativity will allow you new ways to use your tools.

Be a sponge and absorb everything you can from books, mentors, coaches, speakers, and teachers. Know the source that you are getting your information from. Make sure you are getting your advice and coaching from someone who is where you want to be. Do not reach down or to the side—reach up. Do not get your advice or knowledge from someone that is doing worse or is on the same level as you; reach up and learn from those who are where you want to be. Continue to reach for new heights. Always be absorbing knowledge, and continue to evolve, and you will succeed.

## Just Be

> *"To be or not to be? That is the question."*
> *– William Shakespeare*

That is the question we should all ask ourselves. What are you? A human-being, or a human-doing? While we must DO things, to take action, we find that we are always busy, going from one thing to the next, always doing something non-stop. While it seems that we may be productive because we appear to be busy, the truth is that it is only an illusion.

There was once a competition held between two gentlemen, to see who could cut down a tree the fastest with an axe. A young strapping lad would compete against an old man. The young guy looked at the old man and smirked, as if saying, "Yeah, right, there is no way this old man will beat me; I am definitely going to win." The old man just looked at the young man, and said, "Good luck to you, sir." "Luck?! ...I don't need luck," said the young man with a smirk. The host of the competition looked at them both. "Are you ready? On your marks, get set, GO!" The young man took off as fast as he could go! With so much speed, he looked like a ninja with an axe. Two minutes went by, and the young man noticed that the old man was just hitting the tree nice and steady, just pacing himself, and then the old man stopped and began to sharpen his axe.

The young man continued, and about five minutes in, the old man finished sharpening and began again, slow and steady. The young man was still going as fast as possible, continuing his ninja style. Then, within seven minutes, a tree comes down—BOOM! The young guy, surprised, turned around. He was shocked and couldn't believe his eyes. The old man knocked the tree down? But how? Well, just like in this story, we find ourselves beating our axes, over and over, until they get dull, and they are no longer working as efficient as they could be. If only we could take the time, like the old man, and sharpen our axes, sharpen our instruments, and our spirit, mind, and body. The old man knew that eventually the blade would get dull, and he would need to sharpen his axe to be more effective, and to secure that each swing would take out a large chunk out of the tree. It's a fast-paced world because we make it that way. Slow down and sharpen your axe, and your spirit, your mind, and your body.

Just be. Many times we are just running our lives on autopilot. Be aware of your unconscious mind.

Now, take a moment to be still, and just be. Be your true self, without any attachments to who you think you are. Let go of the memories of the past, and for a moment, let go of the future that has not arrived yet. Be present, in the here and now. Just be, without any titles, without any ethnicity, without any gender, without any nationality, without any culture—just be, in no space and in no time.

*Art C. Guerrero*

When you have arrived at this place where there is no matter, no energy, no space, and no time, you have arrived to your spiritual universe. From here, you can connect with your true self: your soul. You are not the clothes you wear; you are not the car you drive, nor the job you do. Just be one with yourself, and from here, you will receive the clarity, not only for what you are meant to do, but also for who you are meant to be—to just be.

# Chapter 8

# The Dance of the Heart & Mind

*"Opportunity dances with those already on the dance floor."*
— H. Jackson Brown Jr.

## Balance

It is important to have balance in the dance of life. There are times that we fall, yet it is important to get back up and continue to dance. Remember to smile and have fun while you are dancing and balancing your heart and mind. While in most cases, the mind loves to lead and the heart follows, the dance must flow gracefully. Sometimes the mind loves to dance alone, yet how many times do we find ourselves attempting to solve a problem, thinking and thinking, and asking, "How?" It's not always about ASKING; it's also about LISTENING. What does your heart say? What are you feeling? Sometimes you get the feeling that something feels right, and sometimes you don't feel good about it.

*"Neurocardiologists have found that most of the cells of the heart are actually neural cells, not muscle cells as was previously believed."* — Joseph Chilton Pearce

In other words, there is a second brain in our heart, a second nervous system. Studies have shown that every time the heart pounds, it emits an electric magnetic pulse (EMP) that goes out about thirty feet. Meanwhile, the brain's EMP only goes out about two inches. The heart is very powerful; therefore, we must pay attention to it. The heart wants to live a meaningful life, create something beautiful, and take risks. You could say that this is where our inner child lives. Our head is where the adult lives, telling us to act right, to be mature, and fit in. This is where the balance of the two are very important. We have responsibilities, and we must also have fun and play. I remember working so much, and working two, and even three, jobs at one point. I was so overworked that I didn't even remember the last time I had taken a vacation. I kept working, wanting to be a responsible adult, and meanwhile, my inner child, with his arms crossed, cried out, "What about me!" We all know what happens when you ignore a child for too long; he will eventually throw a fit. Then my inner child surfaced, and I said to myself, "It's been so long since I have actually had a real vacation, and I'm talking about just visiting family on my time off. It's time to do something fun, something for me." Then I went overboard on my expenses, treating myself to a luxurious vacation; and then, the following month, I realized I might not have enough to cover my bills. Balance work and play, and remember to have fun. We all have an inner child inside. Stop being so busy making a living that you don't remember to live your life.

There must be balance in all areas of your life. On the next page is a picture of the **LIFE WHEEL**.

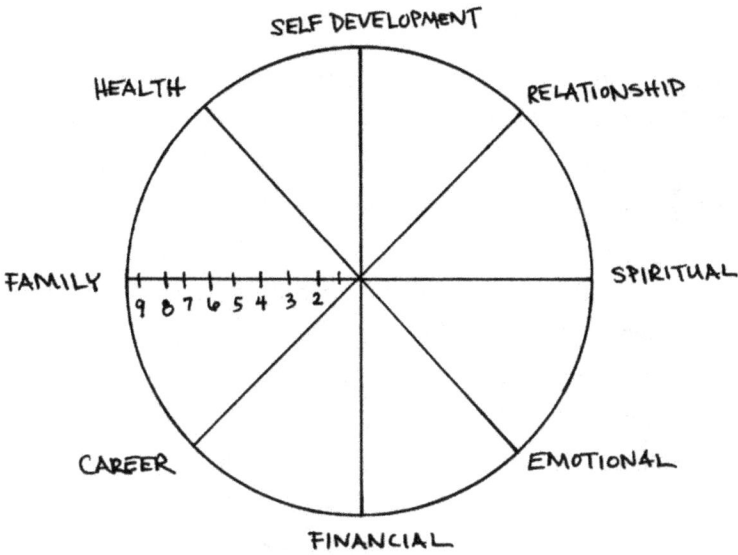

(Visit *ucsuccess.com* to download a PDF copy of LIFE WHEEL.)

Now, on a scale from 1–10, how fulfilled are you in each of these areas?

What would a fulfilling life look like in each area? By evaluating where we are on the life wheel, we can determine which areas need improvement. Some areas have more of our focus than others. Find the two areas that need the most work, and begin to work on improving those areas. Remember, we all have the same 24 hours a day; it's all about balance.

*Art C. Guerrero*

## Thoughts and Feelings

A friend once asked me for relationship advice. He said, "How do I know if this is the right girl, the right relationship? Do I listen to my head or my heart?" In the moment, I replied, "Listen to your head. Logically, does it make sense? Your heart will play tricks, because emotions come and go." Later, I thought about what I said, and I realized that both the mind and the heart must be in sync. I called and told my friend, "It has to make sense in both your head and heart." For an example, in some relationships, the significant other is great at home with his or her partner, yet does not get along with the family. In other cases, they get along great with family and friends, but are just putting on an appearance that everything is great, while at home, the couple may be fighting. It has to be great in public and at home.

Affirmations are great and can work, yet I believe that it is more than just saying affirmations and thinking about what you want to manifest in your life. You must feel and believe the affirmations with your heart as well. When you speak to the Universe, she will listen. I say *she* because it's not about what you say, it's how you say it. Feel what you say. Be aware of the emotions you put behind the words you say. E-motion is energy in motion. Your feelings and emotions send out energy. This energy can also be translated as a frequency. Your vibe attracts your tribe. When we send out a certain energy, a certain frequency, anything on that same radio wave will be listening, and we will attract it to us and bring it into our lives. If our lives are not the way we want them to be, then it's time to self-evaluate our emotions, and change our frequency.

Our thoughts allow us to be aware of our unconscious. Our body is part of our unconscious. The body learns and has reflex responses to protect itself from a similar danger it may encounter in the future. Yet as conscious beings, we can train, prepare, and fine tune our instruments, our bodies. The mind is powerful and can say, "I believe and have the willpower to run a marathon." Yet we must still train and prepare our body for the run.

Similarly, in our mind, we say, "I will change, I will take action, and I will work on my life wheel. I will eat healthier, workout, work on my finances, work on my relationship, etc." Yet are we training and preparing ourselves for the journey? Have we taken a course, read a book, learned a new skill? Do we have the right gear? Like in my motorcycle accident, I had some of the gear, but not all; yet I was still able to get back up and keep going. I had the motorcycle jacket that had the shoulder pads, elbow pads, and spine pad. Looking at the jacket now, I am grateful and glad I was wearing it. If not, I would have shattered my shoulder and elbow. I was also wearing motorcycle gloves that had metal plates that protected my knuckles. If it weren't for that protection, my hands would have been shattered. As an artist, it could have been devastating. You don't have to have all the right gear; just have some gear, to be prepared.

Our thoughts help us to prepare and plan, and our hearts tell us it's time to get out of our heads and into our lives. Feel excited; you are on your way to a new life.

*Art C. Guerrero*

## Music & Atmosphere

We must be willing to dance to the beat of a different drum. Many times, we are dancing to someone else's music, and living someone else's life or dream. Listen to the music that your mind is playing, and the beat that your heart is drumming. By living our lives with what is most meaningful to us, we will gladly dance with our hearts, which will give us goosebumps and rage, so that we will self-actualize.

If I were to ask you where your life is on a scale from one to ten, what would you say? Most would say about a seven. Most people live their lives anywhere between a six and an eight. That's because they are being aware of their behavior, depending on the environment, based on their exterior world, and are wanting to fit in. Think about it. If you said you were living at about a four, not feeling good about your life and being depressed, most people (6–8 on the scale) would encourage you to keep your head up, and they would motivate you. Yet when you are wanting to grow and evolve to a nine or ten, to better your life, people (from a 6–8) try to bring you down to their level, saying, "I don't know if you want to do that. Are you sure? It seems risky; are you really ready for that?" They say this because they are coming from the mentality of a level six through eight.

Great heroes of history have shown us that they lived in alignment with something within themselves, living from their heart and connecting to their spiritual universe. Know your passion, and pay attention to the things that bring you joy, and to the things that cause you rage. The things that cause you rage do so because something you

## The Art of Unconscious Success

value, and is important to you, has been violated. Be mindful and listen to your heart. Your heart connects you to your spirit, and to your soul.

What fills your heart with passion and love? Music will play, but it's not until you hear *your* song play that it will connect to your heart and make you dance with joy and excitement.

> Music plays, as joy fills our hearts,
> Sunny days, a new love affair starts,
> Heart and mind now together as one
> Dancing to the beat of my own drum.
>
> What moves you, what stirs your soul
> What grooves you, will you lose control
> Live and laugh, always proceed with love
> And you will have success from above.
>
> – Art C. Guerrero

Have awareness of the passion and love that comes from deep within. Living with all that rings true to your core, will allow you to flow gracefully through your life, having an amazing dance between the heart and mind.

## Communication

Do you know that there are three parts to the way we communicate, and that a major part of our communication is done unconsciously? Have you ever heard or told someone, "Did you not hear what I just said? Am I not communicating correctly?"

Studies have shown, and Neuro-linguistic programming (NLP) teaches us the three ways we communicate…

- 7% words – all we use for communication, and is only surface meaning.
- 38% tone – our tone of voice, which has deep meaning.
- 55% body language – posture, hand gestures, expressions.

Now, if words are only 7%, that is probably why we tend to misinterpret text messages or emails. At least with picking up the phone and hearing someone's voice, we can communicate a lot clearer. For example, if I have a sad and depressing tone of voice, and I say, "I'm having a wonderful day," versus saying the same sentence in a cheerful upbeat tone, the meaning translates differently. They are the same words but just with a different tone.

If I am planning on having an important conversation, I would rather communicate with that individual in person, face to face. That way, we are both communicating at 100%, including body language. Most men only listen to the words and are not as aware as most women, who intuitively understand the three parts of communication; which is why most men miss the clues that women are trying to give them. We usually hear them say, "It's not what you said; it's how you said it."

Be aware of the tone; when words have a rising pitch, it is interpreted as a question. When the pitch is level and stays the same, it is a statement. When the pitch descends, this is interpreted as a command.

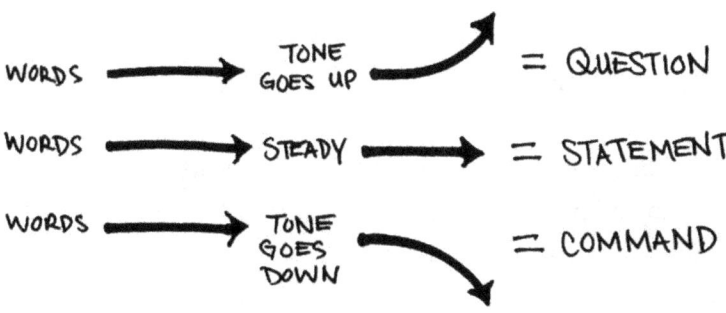

In becoming a great communicator and building rapport, it is great to match and mirror body language and tone (very subtly). Also, if you notice the other person is using a certain phrase or certain words they prefer, when you use the same words, they will feel like they know you and that you have things in common. People like people who are like them, or people whom they would like to be like. The person with the most flexibility will succeed.

When we are mindful of our tone and body language, we will have more awareness of our unconscious communication. Most people focus on the use of the words, and are not always aware of the communication that is happening on the unconscious level—the message that is still being received unconsciously. Your mind is saying the words, and your heart (body) is communicating with tone and body language. Be aware of your communication, at 100%, and the mind and body will dance gracefully as you communicate. Now you have another tool that you can use, to have unconscious success.

## Health & Wellness

The body and heart needs to be healthy; as mentioned before, we must train and prepare our body. By staying fit and healthy, the body can operate at an optimum level, and be more efficient and productive. When we do not eat right, our bodies won't have the energy required to build up our immune systems to fight disease. If we do not sleep properly, our bodies are unable to recharge, repair, and rebuild properly while we sleep. There is a reason we are meant to have six to eight hours of sleep a night, for at least a quarter of our lives, if not a third of our lives. The body is an amazing instrument, yet we must also take care of our bodies. It is the temple of our spirit, of the soul.

Some people will say, "I don't like vegetables," even though they know they are good for them. Now, why don't you like them? You just don't? No, something in your unconscious mind has convinced you of this. If you really ask the question, you might be surprised why it's telling you this. Think of when you were a child—did you eat your vegetables? Did your parents eat their vegetables? Someone you looked up to said with a lot of passion, "I hate vegetables!" And for some of you that love vegetables, your parents and loved ones ate vegetables.

There is something in your unconscious mind that has led you to take on the belief that you do or don't like something, whether it's eating healthy, exercising, or reading books. Why would you wait until life hits you with a ton of bricks, or the doctor tells you something very serious has to change? Many want to change, yet they find it challenging. Really look at your wellness, mentally and physically.

When someone is not doing well, and is not healthy, we find that it's usually because they are not eating healthy, not exercising, or not resting or sleeping enough. At one point in my life, I had sleep apnea and had to use a CPAP machine. I had high blood pressure and was overweight—okay, who am I kidding; I was a bit obese. I told myself that I would never go over a certain weight limit, and one day, I got on the scale, took a deep breath (as if that was going to help make me lighter) and, "OH, NO!" I was one pound away from hitting the weight limit I promised myself I would never go over. Something had to change.

The first thing I did was call someone that had reached their fitness goal, to find out where I needed to start. I had tried to change in the past, and I had tried to do it by myself, but I was unsuccessful. I realized that I would require a coach or mentor. My coach was a friend of mine, yet I knew he would hold me accountable. Support is essential in personal transformation. My coach advised me that in order to reach my goal, it was 80% nutrition and only 20% exercise. If I was not going to eat heathy, the workout would be pointless. He also told me it was important to get plenty of rest, so that my muscles could recover and rebuild properly. WOW! Good to know. I wrote down my end goal, my weekly goal, and my daily goal. I started my workout, and in the first month, I dropped 17 pounds, and by the end of the three-month workout program, I was down 35 pounds and in the best shape of my life. I went to get a checkup with my physician, and he told me that my blood pressure had normalized, and that I no longer had sleep apnea. I smiled from ear to ear.

I was feeling physically fit and healthy, yet I also felt I was not living a fulfilled life, and that something was missing. I began to look at my mind in the same way as my body: nutrition, rest, and exercise.

- **Nutrition** – What would that be? Knowledge, books (audiobooks), classes, and seminars.

- **Resting** – This is not only about sleeping. I would also make sure to slow down and not have my mind in work mode all the time. Find time to interrupt the thinking mind, and just relax, with no distractions; relax, meditate, listen to calm nature sounds, whether it's with headphones or actually being in nature and being still.

- **Exercise** – Yes, exercising the mind by applying the new knowledge, and doing reps and continuous practice of what I learned, to instill the habit and to expand the mind.

Stretching the mind is as vital as stretching your muscles every morning. I used to wake up and just go. GO, GO, GO. It wasn't until I pulled a muscle and hurt my body that I started stretching every morning. Think about it. Even animals stretch: cats, dogs, etc. Anytime they wake up or have just been lying down for too long, they will get up and stretch. Yet humans don't always remember to stretch. Get the blood flowing to every part of your body, and prepare every muscle for the unexpected adventurous day you are about to have. Similarly, things in life happen unexpectedly, and if we are not mentally prepared to handle it, we freak out! The more you learn, the more tools you will have, and even though you might not always need each tool, when you need it, you'll have it. It's better to have it and not need it, than need it and not have it. Better yet, if you have it, use it.

The mind will expand and make new neuro connections every time we learn something new. The brain creates new cells as we learn something new. Those that age faster do so because there are no new cells being generated. They are not learning anything new, and like a tree, if we are not growing, we're dying (not living).

Life can be tense: tight muscles, tight financially, tight in many areas. Stretching has done wonders for my body and mind. You will not tear or break; stretching will expand your mind and your potential. Prolong your life by living healthy and stretching each day.

Art C. Guerrero

## Energetic Momentum

Motion creates e-motion: energy in motion. Move around, move forward, and keep going. You will succeed, but at what speed?

After my motorcycle accident, someone asked, "What would be the reason you are still alive after falling off a motorcycle and hitting the highway, going 90 mph, with no helmet on?" I sat back in my chair, and replied, "Well, I believe it was the fact that I was going 90 mph, faster than everyone else going 65 mph, which was the speed limit. By going faster, I was able to decrease speed as I slid past traffic, giving the other cars time to slow down. If I had been going the same speed as everyone else, I would have been trampled and run over." How does that show up in our lives, where we are just going the same speed as everyone else around us? When we fall, we get trampled and run over by everyone around us, and we have difficulty recovering. When we are going faster, we are learning as much as possible, and we are still absorbing the knowledge and having personal growth. If we fall or fail, it's okay, because we have come a lot further along in our journey than most. We are able to get back up and keep going. We may fall, while others have not even jumped at the opportunity, or have taken a leap forward in their lives.

Ninety miles per hour may sound like a lot to some, yet the thing to do is to slowly turn the throttle and increase the speed. As you continue to grow and expand, you will be able to have more momentum. I am not saying to go ninety miles per hour; just go a little faster than where you are currently in life. Many of you have coasted through life for too long. To ensure your success, you must pick up the pace. Your time is valuable, so travel with more velocity. Success is a journey; have fun and enjoy the ride.

# Chapter 9

# Realize & Utilize

**Stay in Your Lane**

Everyone has their own lane. Maintain yours... there's less traffic and no speed limit.

Everyone has their own talent—the thing they love and are great at. We don't want to be the jack of all trades and the master of none.

I had a lesson that I learned the hard way. When I first bought the print shop, I was very eager to grow our business. All we did in the beginning was commercial printing: everything to do with just paper, business forms, business cards, envelopes, brochures, flyers, raffle tickets, etc. I noticed that at times, we had customers ask us about signs. Since I had previously worked at a sign company in Arlington, Texas, I figured, why not buy a vinyl cutter/plotter machine so we could make decals, small signs, banners, and vehicle graphics? We went ahead and started offering additional products. Then, later that year, we went to an expo, where we purchased a DTG printer (Direct to Garment), which was very cool, because we could print full color, photo quality images on T-shirts. It was very different from a screen printed T-shirt; it was a very high quality T-shirt. Now we were offering more products. Many of our customers were happy that we could offer more products in one location: the one-stop shop.

Well, while that sounded like a good idea, and we did that for about three years, our sales were about the same as our previous years. There was no big change. The only thing that was different was that I found myself busier, yet there was no major increase in sales. I was putting in more hours for the same pay. Something did not add up.

I started to look at our business a little differently. I was analyzing: What percentage of our business was commercial printing? What percentage was T-shirts? And what percentage was signs and decals? We realized that T-shirt printing and signs was only 15 percent of our entire sales. We decided to eliminate the T-shirt printing, stop making signs, and sell those machines. We focused on the 85% of the business that the company was known for doing for the last 11 years: commercial printing. We focused on what we were already great at, and professional at. We also invested in that side of the business. We upgraded our printers and went from off-set printing to digital printing. Now, with the new printers and our undivided attention to paper printing (commercial printing), we became faster and more efficient. Customer satisfaction was at its best, and word spread. There's nothing like word of mouth.

In the first year that we started focusing on what we were great at, our business grew, and our sales were significantly higher. We had our best year in the history of our company. We stayed in our lane, not only doing what we do best, but also improving our skill and talent— sharpening our skill (sharpening our axe).

There are many things that we can do, yet we must ask ourselves, "Is it something we love to do, and is it worth our time?" I feel that I am a great graphic designer, yet it eats up a lot of my time, where I could be focusing on sales or improving production. I began to delegate more, and with a smile, started referring customers to other graphic designers. I also began referring customers to other sign companies and T-shirt printing companies. While that seemed as if I was giving business away that could have been mine, I also understood the law of reciprocity, and how karma and the Universe work. Even if those companies did not refer customers to me, the Universe would return the favor.

Stay in your lane, master your skill, and you will succeed.

## In Your Favor

Life doesn't happen TO us; it happens FOR us. Yes, even the difficult and challenging things that happen in our lives. Depending on where you are in your life, this can be a little bit hard to swallow. When a horrible thing happens, it's actually a challenge, and a teaching moment—life teaching us a new lesson. The lesson will continue to present itself until we learn and can grow from it. You'll go through it, until you grow through it.

There are things in life that happen, and sometimes we want to ask, "Why is this happening?" We are not able to understand it in the moment, yet as time passes, and the pieces of the puzzle begin to fall into place, it is then that we can step back and see the bigger picture. "Oh, that's why that happened!" It begins to make sense. There are things that we have asked the Universe to help us manifest, and the Universe is putting the pieces together for us. There are things that are no longer meant to be there, and the Universe is beginning to eliminate those things that no longer serve us. Sometimes it's friends or family that are no longer on the same path (wave length or frequency) that we are on. We wonder why that person hasn't called or come by anymore. Maybe they would distract or derail you from your goal. Let them go. New people and new opportunities will begin to come into your life. Everything is happening for a reason.

A client of mine had been upset that her dad left them when they were very young. Her dad was a womanizer and abandoned her mother and siblings. She was holding on to this grudge against her dad for many years. He had tried to ask for forgiveness, years later after they had grown, yet she could not understand why this happened to her and her siblings. I told her that everything happened the way it was meant to. If she did not go through those difficult times, she might not have fought so hard to become the amazing and successful woman she is today. She and her husband own their own business, and they travel all over the world.

I shared with my client the experience of my stepchildren. While they wished that their parents would have worked things out and stayed together and not split up, they know that their parents aren't arguing and are a lot happier. My step kids have a stepdad that loves and cares for them. They are very happy that their mom has found true love, and they have never seen their mom this happy and in love.

While we want things to happen the way we want them to, the Universe knows what our hearts want. All of our emotions are leading us back to love. Everything that is happening is tipping the scale to bring balance, and to bring us back to love.

There are signs everywhere. Will you keep ignoring them, or will you listen to them?

There's a story of a man that was in a flood. He climbed on top of his house, prayed, and cried to God to save him from the flood. The rain kept pouring, and the water continued to rise and rise. Later, a man came by in a boat and asked him to get in the boat. The man on the house said, "It's okay; God is going to save me." Later, a helicopter came by to rescue him. The man also told the helicopter rescue team, "It's okay; God is going to save me," as if he expected God to literally extend his hand from the sky and save him. How many signs will it take before life has to smack us in the face, for us to wake up?

I remember a time when I hurt my back and was in serious pain, and I sat around immobilized for a week. I asked why this happened and what I could learn from this. As I began to analyze, I realized that I had asked the Universe for something to really shake me up and give me a hard push toward my goals. Wow, I asked for it. What did I learn? Well, for starters, to be more specific and clear in what I wish for. I also learned to take care of my body better, and the experience also allowed me to work on my book and get more writing done. Life is happening FOR me.

There is a reason for everything, and it's all happening in your favor.

## Revisit Your Story

For a moment, look at your story, as just a story. What is the story you're telling, not just to others but to yourself? Your story is not just for you. Your story can also benefit someone else.

Learn from other people's mistakes, because you will never live long enough to make them all yourself. One can grow at a much faster pace by learning from others as well. The story that happens around you, is happening for you. If you are the main character of a certain story, then the story is meant for you to pay closer attention. Everything and everyone in your life is there, or has been there, for a reason, and to teach you something.

A memory is a story: our version of what has happened. What happens, in many cases, is that we have told the same story over and over, so many times that we have convinced ourselves that it is the truth; when in actuality, it is only our perception, our point of view of the story. Many times, we stay in the same situation, in the same cycle, going in circles, because we continue to tell the same story. This happened to me because of this or that. I am (_____) because of it. Do not let a version of the story define who you are. You are much more. In this life, you are the main character of the story; you are the narrator, the director, and the executive producer. You are the one that funds your movie, your story.

What happens in the story, happens for you to evolve; it happens for you to grow from it. The challenges one faces are also lessons for others; therefore, share your story. Things will happen; how you respond to what happens is up to you. You decide where you take the story from there. It's like when the art professor gives you a paper with a scribbled line already on the paper, and he tells you to draw something from that. Life acts in the same manner: when things come your way, you maneuver and dance your way around them.

Every great hero in history goes through a similar path. At some point in our lives, we have and will take a similar journey. As we live the story of our lives, we will be called to action and to an adventure, and we will face a new challenge. We sometimes refuse the call, and continue to stay in the same cycle. Once we have accepted the challenge, we will need guidance and advice from a mentor to be able to cross the threshold. Once we cross into the unknown, the point of no return, we will be tested and face trials. We will form alliances who will assist us in the journey, gaining knowledge and new skills. Personal growth, as well as spiritual growth, will occur (inner change). As we face the challenge (the ordeal), we will be ready to face it, armed with new skills and tools. We will overcome and become a new person from the experience, receiving revelations, atonement, and new treasures, bringing our new gifts and lessons back to the world we know, and back home. We can now face and overcome our daily challenges in the ordinary world, and with the new skills and knowledge, overcome our challenges in the real world.

By taking the path of the hero's journey, this will lead us to self-discovery and living a fully realized life. This path happens in many stories throughout history, cultures, movies, and books. This must happen to obtain self-transformation.

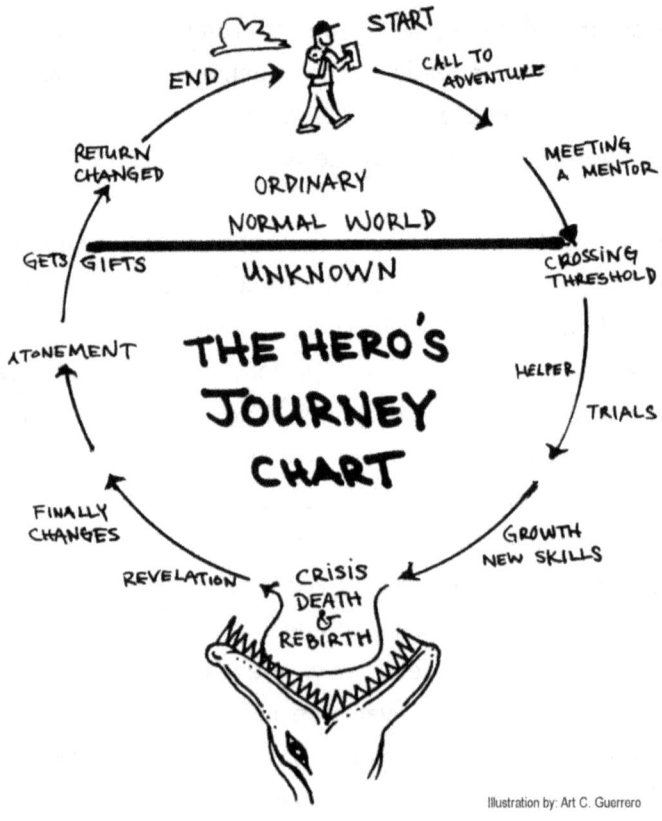

Illustration by: Art C. Guerrero

(Visit ucsuccess.com to download a PDF copy of illustration.)

Revisit your story; what have you learned from your journey? We all know someone that is always reminiscing and telling the same story over and over. We want to continue to take on new challenges, have new adventures, and create NEW stories. Talk about your new, current adventures and lessons. Change your story and change your life.

## Resources

What resources do you have, and what resources do you need? What are all the skills, knowledge, and tools that you have obtained thus far? What are the resources that you have internally, and also what resources do you have externally? It is not always what you know, but also who you know—someone that can help you, mentor you, coach you, or point you in the right direction.

Many times, we have resources that we might not be utilizing: a book we have not read, a documentary we have not seen, a mentor we have not contacted. Every great leader and hero has received assistance and has asked for guidance, yet many people choose to try to do everything by themselves. Utilize all your resources. Mentors and other individuals are willing to assist you in acquiring new resources. We just have to be willing to ask.

One of my mentors once told me, "When you ask for money, you get advice. When you ask for advice, you get money." This was indeed the case for me. I once asked how I could make more money, and I was given advice. I asked for advice and was advised to read more books on personal growth, business, and wealth. Now I have a library of books, a great resource that I have acquired. Some of these books have led me to take courses where I met instructors, speakers, and mentors. I asked them for advice, and by applying their knowledge and wisdom, it has allowed me to make more money and obtain more success in many areas of my life.

Remember to be in a state of awareness and, many times, the Universe will show you a sign. A situation can happen around you that may teach you something new. You might learn something from someone else's conversation. Someone may mention a resource that you may need and can acquire.

Someone once asked, "How can I help more people and make more money in the process?" Many times, if we just listen, people will tell us something they are complaining about, which is a problem for them or for someone else. If you can solve that problem, you can help someone, and when you decide to charge for your service, you will profit as well—creating a win-win situation.

Be aware of the resources you have, and the resources you need, and be ready to receive new resources.

You have three basic tools you can utilize:

- **Personal tools** – Knowledge is power. What have you learned, what are you capable of, and what talents and skills do you have?

- **Social tools** – This not only applies to social media; you also have friends, family, and mentors that you can ask for assistance and guidance.

- **Physical tools** – Books, films, equipment, machines, computers, vehicles, property—anything tangible that can be used as a tool.

## The Power of Words

Words are very powerful. Some people don't realize how strong words really are. I remember, as a young child, when other kids would say, "Sticks and stones may break my bones, but words will never hurt me." The fact is that sticks and stones, in most cases, only affects the physical universe. We might bleed or break our bones, but we will heal. Words usually affect the spiritual universe, our inner self. It's not so much what others say, but what we tell ourselves.

Many individuals believe that they are not good enough, and that they are just okay, and they are okay with just being okay.

In the past, I have felt that I might not be good enough to succeed in writing a book. In school, writing was my worst subject. I had to retake tests and just barely passed my writing class, yet that did not stop me from writing songs or writing poetry. Many of my songs and poetry were just for me. I would write from the heart and express my poetic talent, but because I had not done so well in writing, I did not pursue a professional career. I had friends tell me that I should write a book. I would just say okay, but I didn't think much about it.

Later in life, I went to a seminar and heard a great speaker by the name of Raymond Aaron, talking about writing your book, sharing your story, and branding yourself. I listened to his story about when he wrote a book, and how others have written books, even though they were not great writers when they started. They still wrote, and they have become best sellers, and even *New York Times* best sellers. Zig Ziglar once said, *"You don't have to be great to start, but you have to start to be great."*

We must select our words carefully, externally and internally. I remember saying, *everything is going great, but something is bound to happen*, and guess what? It did. I had even written a song, called "Rollercoaster 99," believing that life is a rollercoaster—there are ups and downs. When everything was going great, I would believe and get ready for something to bring me down. Later, I realized that I was creating what would bring me down. I used to believe that if something bad happened in the morning, then that meant I was going to have a bad day. But life does not have to be that way, just because we got up on the wrong side of the bed.

I changed my words and changed my mentality, and it changed my reality. I choose to believe that I am going up and up, growing and always evolving. Things may challenge me, and that's okay. These things are there to help me grow, to make me stronger for the next challenge that I will face, to advance to the next stage in life.

Say things in the way that you want them to happen. Studies show that your unconscious mind does not process negative words, like no, don't, can't, won't, etc. If I say, "Don't think of a pink elephant." Guess what? You are now thinking of a pink elephant, because it has been brought to your awareness, and you can't help but think of a pink elephant.

I once told myself, "I should pack those shoes tonight. I don't WANT TO FORGET THEM. It's okay, I won't FORGET THEM." Then, the next day, I was at the airport, and I realized that I FORGOT THEM. I programmed my unconscious mind without knowing. So how could I have said it differently? I could have said, "I WILL REMEMBER to pack those shoes; it's okay, I will REMEMBER them.

We do this without thinking about it and then wonder why certain things happen. Like when we tell kids, "Watch out! You are going to SPILL that drink; you are going to SPILL THAT DRINK!" What happens? They SPILL the drink, and you tell the kid, "What did I tell you?" That happened because we told them it was going to happen. When I became aware of this, I began to change and choose my words carefully. In the beginning, it can be challenging, yet if you take your time, it will become easy and effortless to say things in the way you want them to happen. I began to tell my toddler, "BE CAREFUL ...with your drink," BE CAREFUL ...watch your step. Be careful. I've noticed great results by selecting my words carefully, at home, in my personal life, and in business.

We also want to say things in the present tense. Instead of saying, "I want to be successful," say "I'm successful," or instead of saying, "I want to look good," say, "I look good."

By saying you want to do something, or by saying you will get there, it indicates that you are not there yet. I know you may feel that you are not there yet, but the truth is, in most cases, you are already there—you just haven't realized it. Your unconscious mind does not understand the concept of time. It does not know that your present thought is in the past or future. Create your reality in the NOW, in this present moment, and believe that you are already successful. Because you are amazing, wonderful, and successful. You are whatever you say you are, and whatever you believe you are.

## Talents and Gifts

You have talents and gifts, skills you have learned, and knowledge you have gained. You have a story to be told. You have resources at your disposal. You have your words. There are many tools that you can utilize for your benefit. As life happens, utilize each experience to your advantage.

When we become aware of our life experience externally, as well as internally, knowing that it is all happening for us, to prepare us and give us resources, we see life from a different perspective, having more clarity and knowing we are swimming with the current of life.

There is a story of two swimmers: an amateur and a professional. There was a contest to be held. The swimmers would stand at opposite ends of the lake. The professional would swim against the current, and the amateur would swim with the current. The contest would be to see who would reach the opposite end of the lake first. Ready, set, go! The swimmers took off and began to swim, both eager to win. Who do you think won the contest—the professional or the amateur? The amateur won. Why? Because he was swimming with the current. Even though the amateur was not a strong swimmer, the fact that he went with the current, assisted him in winning.

*The Art of Unconscious Success*

Many times, we try to fight the current, going against it. The Universe will show us something, and we think we know better. Life slaps us in the face, and yet we still don't listen. Remember that life is happening FOR you. The Universe is showing us signs, pointing us in the right direction to go with the current. Going with the current means to utilize your talents and gifts. Do what you are great at, and continue to get better at it. Become a master at it. Follow your heart and your passion, and you will win, and you will succeed.

# Chapter 10

# Enhance Your Life

**P.U.S.H.**

*"P.U.S.H. – **P**roceed **U**ntil **S**uccess **H**appens."*
– Art C. Guerrero

We must always PUSH ourselves. Never get too comfortable. It's okay to rest and recharge, but then get up and keep pushing. You can lead a horse to water, but you cannot make him drink. Someone can show us the way and show us the door, but we are the ones that have to decide and push ourselves to walk through the door.

Proceed, reach success, and proceed to your next level of success. Success is a journey; therefore, we must always PUSH ourselves to a higher level of success. As a student of life, the learning never stops; there is always more to learn, and there's always room to grow.

There is a difference between *pushing away from* and *pushing toward* something. In the past, I had told myself that I did not WANT TO BE OVERWEIGHT, and I was focusing on what I did not WANT TO BE. Notice the capitalized words, and remember that your unconscious mind is listening to everything but the negative words.

In the sentence above, you can see that I was focusing on *"I want to be overweight."* This is why it's important for us to have goals, and to have a FOCUS on what we want to PUSH ourselves toward.

Write down your goals: daily, weekly, monthly, and annual goals. What are you striving for? If you don't aim at anything, *"you'll miss 100% of the shots you don't take."* (quote by Wayne Gretzky, Hockey Hall of Famer)

Anything is possible. Everything, at one time, was impossible, until someone did it. Find your passion and go for it. Your daily goals are important because, even if it seems like you are taking a small step, the truth is that you are moving forward. Each goal is a victory to celebrate.

By celebrating each of your goals achieved (big and small), this creates a snowball effect, giving you more energy and fueling you for your next goal. This positive energy will give you more momentum and give you a great push in achieving your next goal. Even when celebrating the wins of others, karma will return that energy toward you by being on the frequency to win and succeed.

Analyze and continue to evolve from each step you take, from each goal you achieve, and proceed forward.

## The Power of Connection

It is one thing to communicate with someone but another thing to make a real connection. To have meaningful relationships in your life means to make real connections. This is more than just making eye contact; it's about making a connection with the heart.

Relationships are everywhere. I am not only talking about the relationship with your significant other, fiancé, or spouse. I'm talking about the relationship you have with your children, siblings, parents, and other family members. What about the relationship with your co-workers, your boss, or your friends? How are you connecting with people? Are you making meaningful connections, or are they superficial? I've learned to have better connections, by opening my heart and being vulnerable. Vulnerable!? Yes, there is great power in being vulnerable. This allows you to be transparent, truthful, and authentic. The greatest connection that one can have is the respectful relationship that you have with yourself—being totally honest with yourself, about who you are, where you are, and where you want to go. One must first know where they are to know which direction to take.

Someone calls you and asks you for directions, and they just say, "How do I get to your location?" Without them telling you where they are, you cannot tell them east, west, north, or south. Know where you are first. What have been your intentions that have led you to where you are in life at the moment? What are the intentions you want to have for your life that will lead you to a new path and have what you want in your life?

Ask. Just ask. The Universe will give you feedback. Once I was at an airport, and while I was in the security check line, I overheard a gentleman on the phone. He was complaining how he was about to miss his flight, because his flight was already boarding, and there were about 30 people in front of him before he could even get past the security check point. He said, "Dang! There is nothing I can do; I'm going to miss my flight." I turned around, as he was three spaces behind me, and I got his attention. Before I could even say a word, he said in a sad tone, "It's okay, man; I'm going to miss the flight." I looked at him, smiled, and waited a second to connect with him. Then I told him, "Breathe, you are going to make the flight. Here's what you are going to do. Go to the front of the line and tell that person your situation, and they will let you pass. Then you will make your flight." He told me, "I don't know if they will." I said to him, with confidence and still smiling, "Just ask... just ask." He looked to the front of the line and looked back at me, and said, "Okay." He made his way to the front of the line, and with sincerity, told that person that his flight was already boarding, and asked if he could please pass. The person in front of the line answered quickly, and said, "Sure, of course." That's what I understood by reading their lips. The gentleman that was rushing to catch his flight looked back at me and said, "Thank you," with the utmost sincerity and appreciation. There was a true connection. I knew that he would get home to his family and tell them the story of the man that told him to *"just ask."*

We never really know what can happen when we JUST ASK. When we don't ask, the answer is always no. When you ask with your heart, genuinely, the answer is usually yes. I recently said to my stepson, Felix, "I want you to know that I love you. I want you to be comfortable telling me if there is something that I need to work on as a father—something that you want me to stop doing, start doing, or keep doing. Give me feedback on how I can be a better father." He smiled and said, "You are doing a great job. I love you, Dad." This filled my heart with joy as we hugged.

Ask, and you will know where you stand. Many times, even in business, when you listen to your customers, business partners, and employees, they will give you feedback. This allows us to know where we are and which direction we should take to improve our business, customer service, and our life. You may know where you are, yet where do you stand with others, and how do they see you in their eyes? Make a real meaningful connection. Be willing to open your mind and heart, and ask.

It is not about having perfect connections or perfect relationships. It's about being authentic, and having authentic connections and relationships. People don't talk about how perfect someone's relationship is; they talk about how authentic it is, and how they have a real connection to each other. In a long-term relationship, many times, the couple can communicate without words. They just look at each other and know what they are thinking, because the connection is on a deeper level. They are connecting at the heart and soul of one another. Remember earlier in the book, when we mentioned how words are only 7% of communication? Pay attention to the other 93%. (Body language is 55%, and tonality is 38%.)

What is the energy, emotion, and frequency that you are resonating at? What are you attracting into your life? If there are new things you want to attract into your life, change the way you connect, your body language, and your energy, and resonate at a higher frequency. Connect on a deeper level in all of your relationships, personal and business. The power of connection also means to connect others to sponsors, like-minded individuals, and resources. This will assist them in achieving their dreams, as well as you achieving yours. You have the gift to make meaningful and powerful connections.

## Desire to Inspire

> *"The best and most beautiful things in the world cannot be seen or even touched; they must be felt with the heart."*
> – Helen Keller

Many of us want to be inspired, and we love it when someone uplifts us, yet what are we doing to inspire others? When we inspire others, we are being at CAUSE instead of living at EFFECT. Some people just complain how life happens to them, and that is why they are where they are at. When we live at CAUSE, we change the dynamics of our life. We are the change. Many people want to change the world, yet they are not willing to change themselves.

What does it mean to inspire? The definition is to fill someone with the urge or ability to do or feel something, especially to do something creative. To create a positive feeling in a person, animate someone with such a feeling. The word comes from the Latin origin, *inspirare*, meaning *to breathe or blow into*.

Therefore, to inspire is to breathe and blow life into someone. At one time in my life, I was just going through the motions, living life how society said I should live, yet feeling empty inside with no real purpose or passion—until I began to get frustrated with the way my life was going, and I decided to do something about it. I was searching for answers and looking for someone to help, so I found mentors, teachers, and authors who began to inspire me. I was getting the creative juices flowing, as I was inspired to create a new life for myself, and to take charge and create my own destiny. Feeling alive again, I reconnected with my passion and found my purpose. Now, more inspired than ever, I wanted to help others by inspiring them to find their passion and find their purpose in life.

As I resonate on the frequency of inspiration, the Universe tends to return the favor and send inspiration in my direction. *Do unto others as you wish to be done unto you.* It becomes an energy source that becomes greater and greater, getting stronger and stronger. The more that I inspire others, the more that life and others inspire me to follow my passion and purpose.

I encourage you to inspire someone today. Inspire someone every day. This will give you tremendous results in your life. I know this from my own experience.

- The first thing you must do to inspire someone is to love what you're talking about. Communicate with passion and enthusiasm. If you are not excited about it, why would others be excited?

- Next, learn the challenges, strengths, and needs of those individuals you want to inspire. Learn who they are, engage, understand, and build.

- The last thing that needs to happen to successfully inspire others: When the individual finds his or her vision, passion, and purpose, the ceiling is raised. Therefore, we must also assist in raising the floor, to raise to their expectations. Do they have the necessary skills and tools to achieve their goals? Are they in the right role and working on the right team? If not, what tools can we give, and how can we assist in strategizing?

Inspire with passion and enthusiasm. Personally engage and support them in realizing their higher purpose in achieving their dream goals.

## Attitude of Gratitude

It is not happiness that brings us gratitude; it's gratitude that brings us happiness.

In everything I do, achieve, and receive, I come from an attitude of gratitude. At times, the things I receive from the Universe are not always what I ask for, yet I know there is a reason the Universe is giving me that challenge (obstacle), and I am grateful for it. To be grateful is to have the readiness to show appreciation and to return kindness.

There is always something to be grateful for. Every morning I wake up, I am grateful, and with a smile, I list the things that I am grateful for: my life, my wife, my kids, my business, the people in my life, and many other things that are currently happening in my life. Do small, random acts of kindness as a sign of gratitude, and the Universe will return the kindness. Smile more, and smile every day. There are times that I remind myself to smile. Even as I sit in silence and observe the world around me, I smile.

One way that my wife shows gratitude and appreciation toward our customers and people in our life is that she gives them compliments. When was the last time you gave a compliment to someone? Give more compliments—genuine compliments—and see the response you will get.

Having an attitude of gratitude toward life will definitely enhance your life. There are many benefits of gratitude. Studies show that gratitude improves your quality of sleep. It's not about the quantity of sleep as much as it is the quality of sleep you will have. In obtaining proper rest, your body will recharge and increase your energy levels, reducing your stress and increasing serotonin. Studies also show that gratitude also decreases blood pressure in those with hypertension.

Gratitude will help you live longer.

Robert Emmons, a professor of psychology at the University of California, elaborated on exactly how expressing gratitude improves our health, in his book, *The Little Book of Gratitude*. Gratitude amplifies the good in our lives, that which we see in others and in ourselves, allowing us to see the positive in what we encounter externally, as well as within our mind, heart, and soul. Gratitude connects us with one another, strengthening and solidifying our relationship with friends, family, and co-workers.

> "As we express our gratitude, we must never forget that the highest appreciation is not to utter words, but to live by them."
> – John F. Kennedy.

Express your gratitude, not just by saying thank you, but also by showing your appreciation to the Universe or God, or the supreme higher source of power that you believe in. Looking at it from a parental or guardian point of view, when a child shows that he or she is grateful for the things they have received, and have utilized those gifts given, the parent or guardian is able to give with more ease and joy to their child, because they know that child will appreciate it, show gratitude, and utilize those gifts. Similarly, we have received gifts and talents, and to show our gratitude, we must use those talents and gifts. We will receive many more gifts, and many more will come in the form of miracles, unexpected phenomenon, and wondrous treasures.

> "We can only be said to be alive in those moments when our hearts are conscious of our treasures."
> – Thornton Wilder

*The Art of Unconscious Success*

There is a story of a man that worked many years at a factory, and after 25 years, he was laid off. The business had some losses and had to release a few of their employees. The next day, he decided to go to his son's swim practice. Later, there was another kid that fell into the water and was drowning, and he jumped in after the kid and saved his life. The man later realized that he was let go from his employment for a big purpose, and he was grateful that he was there the following day, to be of service and save a life.

## Being of Service

*"Being of service is not an option; it is a biological necessity. Every kind of action we do for someone else is a reanimation of our own life force, and of the other person's."*
– Caroline Myss

When you take a look at nature, everything works together, receiving and giving back, being of service to something else. As the water falls from the sky, it services the ground and plant life. As the trees grow and bear fruit, they feed the animals. As the animals breathe, they exhale carbon monoxide, which the trees breathe in, and they give off oxygen in return to other living creatures. The cycle of life is about receiving and giving back. We hold on and we let go. Breathe in and breathe out.

*"The best way to find yourself is to lose yourself in the service of others."*
– Mahatma Gandhi

As we connect with others, being of service, we find our passion and purpose, knowing our rightful place in the Universe, and on a spiritual supernatural level, fulfilling our lives with great joy and passion. We all have a purpose and a way to be of service to someone or something—a higher calling.

Being of service and contribution, beyond oneself, keeps our life in balance, from where we can form a great foundation and build our successes upon. To live beyond survival is to contribute beyond ourselves at each level of success. Receiving and giving back creates balance. Success is not about having or making a lot of financial wealth. True success and wealth include having all areas of your live in synchronicity, working together—family, relationships, health, business—everything we talked about in the life wheel.

As we serve others, this will not only show us the outside of ourselves, but also the inner beauty and greatness within ourselves, giving us true fulfillment, continuing to grow, and giving back and being of service to others.

Remember that as we give, it is important to receive, to maintain a balance in life, as others and the Universe give you gifts and return the favor of service. Receive and accept those blessings and treasures. The Universe will also be of service to assist you in achieving more success, which you can share with others.

How are you showing up for others? Many times, people in our personal lives, as well as in business, ask, "What's in it for me?" (W.I.I.F.M.) How can you help them? How can you solve a problem and be a solution for them? How can we add value to others? Adding value is what attracts and retains customers and employees, and maintains relationships. A business that does not create value will eventually fail. In the same way, any relationship, whether in romance, family, or friendship, there must be value being delivered on both ends of the relationship.

Ask yourself how you can be of service and add value to others, and at the same time be able to balance the rest of your life. Only be of service and give what you can afford (financially, emotionally, physically, and spiritually). Remember to have balance. From balance and stability, we can create our foundation to build our successes upon.

**Have Fun and Celebrate**

> *"We don't stop playing because we grow old;*
> *we grow old because we stop playing."*
> *– George Bernard Shaw*

Remember, above all, to have fun. Many have forgotten how to have fun, or do not have enough fun. It's as if someone told them, "Okay, it's time to get serious. We graduate from school, and life happens; it's time to go to work, and be serious at work, and there's no playing around or goofing off. You want to show that you are serious about your work, and that way, you can earn a living and pay your bills!" Wow! Life got too serious too fast—busy at work, busy with life, rush, rush, rush. The average person rarely takes a vacation, and when they do, they decide to take the time to go visit family, and then it's back to work. We must make time to take care of our inner child and have fun.

Studies show that criminality, obesity, and declining creativity is linked to recreational deprivation. Having fun provides nourishment for the brain, body, and spirit.

Having more fun improves our relationships, both in business and in life. Experiencing fun with others has a positive effect on building trust and communication. Having fun offers us an opportunity to connect and be creative. As we laugh together, this sends a message to the brain that says that we have similar values and are alike, allowing us to bond and build rapport with one another. Couples that have fun more often tend to have a happier marriage. Businesses that have fun at work, have proven to have co-workers get along and work better together, creatively finding solutions, and being more efficient and productive.

Fun makes us smarter, improving our concentration and memory, and reducing stress when we immerse ourselves in things we enjoy. Having fun engages us to learn something new. The more you laugh, the more positive emotions and serotonin you will produce; thus, reducing stress, depression, and anxiety. Research shows that stress can have an effect on your immune system and hormones, such as cortisol, insulin, testosterone, and estrogen. It is important to engage in fun physical activities. This is also important in exercise workouts. Be safe and have fun; otherwise, it will just feel like work, and you won't like doing it.

*The Art of Unconscious Success*

When you work hard, you get to play hard. Enjoy life, slow down, and smell the tulips. Laugh at yourself and at things that happen. Life is happening *for* you. Have the intention of having fun, enjoying the journey of success. With every win and accomplishment, remember to celebrate. Celebrate your wins, even the small ones, and the Universe will give you more to celebrate.

I was explaining this concept to my father once, at a kids' pizza place that had video games, as we were celebrating my daughter's 3rd birthday. I told him the importance of celebrating small wins—the little gifts we receive. As soon as I said that, I noticed a penny on the floor. I picked it up, and said, "Yes, thank you, I'm a money magnet!" My father tilted his head and gave me this look, as if to say, "Okay?" as he smiled. Then, as we were walking, I looked over and found another penny. I picked that penny up, and now I was jumping up and down. I said, "Yes, thank you, I am a money magnet!" At that point, he was just laughing. I told him, "When you are grateful and also CELEBRATE, the Universe will give you more." Then I looked down again, and I found two quarters right next to each other. "WOW!" said my father. "That's crazy how that happened." That day, I noticed that the lesson was not only for him as much as it was the Universe showing me how it works with something physically tangible. I've also come to notice how this happens in other areas in my life, celebrating the people in my life, and the opportunities, big and small.

Celebrate your life and each win. Fun will increase your energy, and you will live longer. Remember, whatever you do, have fun. If you are not having fun, then what's the point?

*Art C. Guerrero*

You are the creator of your Universe and your destiny. Have fun creating your success.

# SPECIAL THANKS TO

To my amazing, beautiful wife, **Mireya Guerrero**, who has always supported me and has encouraged me to follow my dreams and achieve success, for us and our family; sharing my story, life lessons, and path to success with my readers, students, and the world. I love you Mireya; you are my best friend and soulmate. I will always love, respect, appreciate, and treasure you forever. Thank you for always reminding me: "Nothing has meaning but the meaning you give it."

To my daughter, **Gia Karina Guerrero**, you mean the world to me; you are my angel and my inspiration. You motivate me to better myself, to ensure I can give you the best tools for you to live your best life. Gia, you inspired me to leave my mark in history, and leave you a book that can guide you and others in the journey to success and ultimate happiness.

To my older kids, **Felix Vasquez** and **Richard** (Tres) **Vasquez**, whom I have always loved as my own children. There are many reasons why the universe has put us in each other's lives. Felix, thank you for the willingness to learn and evolve. You have always made me proud. You have also taught me to evolve and look at life in a whole new light. Richard, I am proud of you and your many accomplishments. You are willing to learn and grow from whatever life throws at you. Keep moving forward. I see a bright future for both of you.

To my parents, **Argelia Guerrero** (Mom) and **Jose Guerrero** (Dad), thank you for always motivating me and telling me that I could do anything I put my mind to. Mom, you have always encouraged me to read books and to think for myself. Mom, you always inspired me as I would see you teach your Sunday school class with so much pride and joy. Dad, thank you for being an example and showing me how to be a leader and public speaker. I always love watching you preach and teach with inspiration and passion.

To my favorite brother, **Josue Guerrero**, thank you for having a big heart and being there when I need you. I am always here for you. Josue, you are an awesome brother. I wish you happiness and success in all your endeavors.

To **Jim Dixon**, I am eternally grateful to you. You have always been a great mentor and role model. Thank you for coaching me and teaching me about business. Thank you for the opportunity and motivation to become an entrepreneur and own my own company.

To **Jon Morgan** and **Kim Morgan**, thank you for being my role models and mentors. Jon, thank you for coaching me and giving me business advice. Jon, you motivated me to get back into reading, and to realize that all millionaires have a library in their homes. Thanks to you, I have my own library of personal development and transformational books. Kim, thank you for being my mom's friend, and for being in our lives in a way that you can't imagine. Both of you have been a great example and inspiration to always remind me to give back and be there for others.

To **Robert Raymond Riopel**, thank you for being an amazing inspirational teacher and mentor, and for coaching me and motivating me to tell my story and to become a public speaker and trainer. Thank you for brainstorming with me as we came up with the title of this book.

To **Roxanne McGhee-Riopel**, thank you for your compassion and motivation. Thank you for showing me what a power couple looks like. You guys have inspired me to live life with passion.

To **Raymond Aaron**, thank you for your lessons and countless teachings. You are an amazing teacher and mentor. I am grateful for the coaching and guidance in becoming the best version of myself. You inspired me to write a book and become a published award winning author.

To **Les Brown**, thank you for your blessing. I am eternally grateful and privileged that you were able to do the foreword for this book. You have motivated and uplifted me to share my story, and have inspired me to step into my greatness and live my dreams.

To **Brigitta Hoeferle**, you are a fantastic success coach and mentor. You have encouraged me, and you always gave me that extra push I would sometimes need to take action and follow my dreams. Thank you for holding me accountable and for motivating me to reach for the stars.

To **Lee Andrew Williams**, you are a magnificent coach and mentor. Thank you for always encouraging me to move from mediocre to magnificent. I always hear you in the back of my mind, asking me, "Where else does that show up in your life?"

To **Christiana Carter-Agnir**, thank you for your coaching and guidance. You have helped me find clarity and remove the mental blocks. Thank you for always believing in me. I'm truly blessed and grateful that you are a part of my life.

To **King Raj Singh**, you have inspired me to grow and achieve my dreams. You have been a great role model for success. Thank you for your friendship and mentorship. I'm looking forward to our many adventures on the stage and off. Thank you for your advice and motivation.

To the amazing group and wonderful people of **21 Secrets Coaching & Mentoring Program**, thank you for your insights that have greatly inspired me to write this book. Every member holds a place in my heart. Thank you **Karyn Mullen, Danielle Stevens, Ahmed Hawari, Biaa Muntean, Karen Carpenter, Lee Downer, Kelly Laughton, Darcy Berger, Anita B. Berger, Yasantha Amal Indi, Chinmai Swamy, Ivy and Ivan Vance**. I love each and every one of you.

To **Emma Aaron**, you are awesome! I love to see young people step into their greatness and become role models for other young adults. You have been an inspiration for my daughter to step into her greatness. Keep learning and evolving into the best version of yourself. I see big things in your future. You are a great shining light for millions. Thank you.

To **Curtis Martin**, thank you for holding me accountable and for motivating me to get my book done. Thank you for being a great friend and being there for me. Your family has always been wonderful and amazing to me. I wish you the best.

To **Steven Sanders**, my childhood friend whom I have known since elementary school, thank you for being an example and stepping into your leadership role. Seeing you write a book and become an author has inspired me to write my book and tell my story.

To **Angel Valles**, one of my best friends who has always been there for me, I always remembered you telling me, "You should write a book." You have inspired and motivated me to tell my story and motivate others. Thank you for all your support and for always believing in me.

To **Nancy Castro**, *the Confidence Catalyst*, thank you for being a shining light. Seeing your journey and your success has inspired me to finish writing my book and become more confident and follow my dreams. You have motivated me to continue to inspire others and step into their greatness and transformation.

To **Michael Stevenson**, thank you for all your teachings and wonderful lessons (blows my mind). You have been a great influence to transform my destiny. You have motivated me to become a published author. It is always an honor to attend your courses and learn from one of the best in the field of NLP.

To **Brent Hilliard**, thank you for being a role model of success, and for inspiring me to follow my dreams. You have motivated me to continue to learn and grow my business.

To **Jerry Morales**, thank you for being a great mentor. Seeing your success and commitment as Mayor of Midland, Texas, and as a business owner, has motivated me to write my book. You have moved me to become successful and know that anything is possible with hard work and dedication. Thanks a million.

To **Dr. Joe Dispenza**, thank you for inspiring me to write my book. Reading all your books has transformed my way of thinking and has enhanced my life. Your courses and lessons have made a profound impact in my life. My family and I thank you from the bottom of our hearts.

To **Dr. Joe Vitale**, thank you for sharing your story. Seeing your success and journey has motivated and encouraged me to continue to improve and become the best version of myself. I love your lessons on *Ho'oponopono*. Thank you for being a major inspiration.

To **Grant Cardone**, thank you for motivating me to be obsessed and not be average. All of your books have made a memorable impact. I love to hear your audiobooks and feel your energy and passion as you read your books. You have motivated me to continue to push myself and become an author. Thank you for your energy, passion, and inspiration!

To **Steve Harvey**, thank you for inspiring me to JUMP. Your books and journey of success have inspired me to write my book. You have motivated me to follow my dreams, act like a success, and think like a success.

To **T. Harv Eker**, your book, *Secrets of the Millionaire Mind*, transformed my life. Thank you for your courses and life lessons that have immensely changed my life. They have been beneficial to my family and myself. I love your quote, *"Successful people have fear, successful people have doubts, and successful people have worries. They just don't let these feelings stop them."* Thank you for being an incredible inspiration.

To **Thomas Tadlock**, thank you for being a leader, coach, and mentor. You have inspired me to write my book and share my story. Thank you for always believing in me. Thank you for being an amazing trainer and teacher. Thank you for always pushing me to advance and step into my greatness.

To **Adam Markel**, thank you for believing in me. Thank you for your tough love, and for inspiring me to write my book and to become the best speaker that I can become. Adam, you have motivated me to pivot and enhance my life. You have been an inspiration, and I have adopted your saying, which I say everyday: "I LOVE MY LIFE!"

To **Dwayne Johnson**, thank you for being an amazing role model and mentor. You've motivated me to continue pushing myself with work ethic. Love your quote: *"Success isn't overnight. It's when every day you get a little better than the day before. It all adds up."*

To **Jack Canfield**, thank you for inspiring me to write my book. I am grateful for your books and life lessons that have influenced me in my journey to success and a fulfilled life. I love your quote: *"If we are not a little bit uncomfortable every day, we're not growing. All the good stuff is outside our comfort zone."*

To **Bob Proctor**, thank you for sharing you knowledge on the subconscious mind. You have been a great inspiration, for me and for my book. Thank you for being the amazing person that you are, and for motivating me to be the best for my family and myself.

To **Tony Robbins**, thank you for being a major inspiration and motivation. You are an outstanding mentor and coach. You have inspired me to transform my life and to continue to reach my peak performance. You have motivated me to write my book and help transform the lives of others. Thank you for being an inspirational mentor.

To **Dr. Nido Qubein**, thank you for being a spectacular example and mentor. You have been a great inspiration and influence, in my life and in my success. You really motivated me when you said, *"If you believe you can, and believe it strongly enough, you'll be amazed at what you can do."* Thank you for teaching me to create more WOW experiences in my life.

To **Rey Perez**, thank you for being a great mentor and inspiration. You have motivated me to write my book and to elevate my personal brand to celebrity status. Thank you.

To **John Assaraf**, thank you for encouraging me to write my book. You inspired me when you said, *"The strongest factor for success is self-esteem: Believing you can do it, believing you deserve it, believing you will get it."* Thank you for being an exceptional mentor.

To **Brian Tracy**, thank you for your inspirational books and teachings. You have inspired me to become a published author. You have been a great mentor. Your lessons have assisted me to become successful in my business and personal life.

To **JP Sears**, thank you for being an inspiration for my book and my success. I love the way you teach and inspire with style. Thank you for your point of view on life. I loved it when you said, *"If you don't like what you're seeing in your life, maybe the highest virtue is to address the one who is seeing your life."*

To **Russell Brunson**, thank you for being an amazing coach and mentor. You inspired me to write my book when you said, *"There are people today that need what you have. They are waiting for you to find your voice so you can help them change their lives."* Thank you for your motivation.

To **Ellen DeGeneres**, you have motivated me to write my book and share my story. You are an inspiration for my family and me. Love your quote, *"It's failure that gives you the proper perspective on success."*

To **Brendon Burchard**, you have inspired me to do what I love, and to be a role model of the energy I wish the world had. You motivated me when you told me, *"You have a chance every single morning to make that change and be the person you want to be."* Thanks a million.

To **Greg Montana**, thank you for being a humble and wonderful coach and mentor. You have inspired me to write my book. Thank you for all your lessons and teachings.

To **Johnnie Cass**, thank you for being an incredible coach and mentor. Thank you for reminding me that I teach others how to treat me, by how I treat myself. You have inspired me to write this book and to continue to reach new levels of success. You have made a memorable impact in my life, and have been a major inspiration to enhance my life.

To **Berny Dohrmann**, Chairman of CEO SPACE, thank you for your coaching and mentorship. You have motivated and inspired me to write this book. Your lessons and advice have made a major difference in the success of my business and my life. Thanks a million.

To **Ken Courtright** and **Bill Courtright**, thank you for being amazing coaches and mentors. Thank you for your advice and teachings. You have inspired me to write this book, and to continue to read books and increase my intellectual property. Thanks a million.

To **Mark Yuzuik**, thank you for being an influence on my success. You are an incredible coach, speaker, and mentor. You have inspired me to continue to grow and evolve to a new level of success. Thank you for being an inspiration, for this book and for my success.

To **Will Smith**, thank you being a great role model and mentor. You have inspired me to make changes in my life and become the best version of myself. You motivated me to write this book when you said, *"Don't chase people. Be yourself, do your own thing, and work hard. The right people—the ones who really belong in your life—will come to you, and stay."*

To **Mileka Lincoln**, thank you for being an inspiration. Your level of commitment, at Hawaii News Now, and your passion and work ethic, has inspired me to reach a new level of success. You have motivated me to follow my dreams, and to write and share my story. Thank you. Aloha.

To **Robert Kiyosaki**, thank you for being a spectacular mentor. Your books and story have inspired me to write this book and share my story. You have motivated and taught me how to obtain success in my business and in life. Thank you.

To **Gerry Foster**, thank you for being a great coach. You have inspired me to swim in blue ocean instead of red ocean. Thank you for the lessons and teachings. You have inspired me to stand out and make my mark in history. Thank you.

To **Marcia Wieder**, my thanks to you and Dream University. You are a fantastic coach, speaker, and mentor. You have motivated me to write this book and share my story and vision, and to continue to help others achieve their dreams and goals. Thank you for your passion and inspiration.

To **Dean Graziosi**, thank you for your teachings and mentorship. Your book, *Millionaire Success Habits*, has impacted my life, and you have been an inspiration. You motivated me to write and become an author. Thank you for your passion and commitment to my success.

To **Lisa Nichols**, your books have being inspirational. Thank you for being an outstanding coach and mentor. Your books and messages have motivated me to continue to achieve new goals every day. Thank you for telling me: *"You are the designer of your destiny; you are the author of your story."* Thanks a million.

To **Coxy Chiara Rodoni**, thank you for being a great inspiration. You have motivated me to always dream big and live life with style. Thank you for being you, and for reminding me to be the best version of myself.

To **Gary Rahman**, thank you for being an awesome friend, and for motivating me to continue to push myself. You have motivated and inspired me to write this book and share my story. Thank you for your advice, friendship, and mentorship.

To **Avital Miller**, thank you for your support and for always believing in me. Seeing your success and journey of becoming a speaker and author has inspired me to write my book and share my story. Thank you for your coaching and motivation.

To **Maureena Benavides**, seeing your level of commitment and compassion, for others and their happiness, has inspired me. Thank you for being there for my family, and for being an inspiration.

To **Dianneth Vasquez**, thank you for being an amazing friend, and for holding me accountable. Thank you for always believing in me. You are a great coach and friend.

To **Maury Ruiz**, thank you for being a great friend, and for encouraging me to follow my dreams. Thank you for pushing me in the right direction. Keep being an awesome warrior, fight for your dreams, and may you reach all of your goals.

To **Anthony Mallett**, thank you for being a great coach and friend. You have always motivated me to push toward my goals, finish my book, and share my story. Thank you for being a great leader.

To **Marcus Sauseda**, thank you for being a great friend and for always believing in me. Keep being a Rhino, and fight for your dreams. Thank you for motivating me and always being there for me, bro.

To **Evelyn Bailey**, thank you for inspiring me to start oil painting again. You have motivated me to express my creativity in all areas, including my writing. Thank you for being a shining light and a great mentor.

To **Gilbert Vara Jr.**, thank you for being an awesome primo, and for always believing in me. You motivated me to know that the only limits I have are the ones I put in front of myself. Thank you for being a great role model and inspiration.

To **Rene Martinez**, thank you for always being there for me and treating me like family. Thank you for motivating me to dream big and to know that anything is possible. Thank you for being an incredible friend.

To **Jacques Godin**, thank you for being a tough coach and mentor. You have always been straight forward with me and have pushed me to better myself. You have inspired me to write this book and share my story with the world. Thanks a million.

To **Carlos Gonzales**, thank you for always being a remarkable friend, and for motivating me to think big. You will always have a place in my heart, and you will always be family. Thank you for believing in me.

To **Mamie Lamley**, thank you for being an outstanding coach and mentor. You have a way with words that are inspiring and compassionate. Thank you for your support and influence to write my book and share my story.

To **Chris Ybarra**, thank you for being an awesome friend and for always believing in me. Thank you for your support and motivation. Thank you for reminding me to always have fun!

**Norma De La O** y **Julio De La O**, Gracias primos por creer siempre en mí. Ustedes han sido excelente ejemplos. Gracias por motivarme a escribir este libro y a alcanzar siempre el siguiente nivel de éxito. Me han inspirado a viajar más y vivir la vida al máximo. Los amo mucho.

*The Art of Unconscious Success*

To **Chris Burns**, thank you for being a fantastic coach and mentor. You have motivated me to write this book and to follow my dreams. Thank you for believing that I have greatness and a story to share with the world. Thank you from the bottom of my heart.

To **Gerardo Grado**, thank you for always believing in me. You have been a remarkable friend and have always been there for me. Thank you for your support and inspiration.

To my awesome friends, **Charles Kenimer** and **Eric Esparza**, thank you for always believing in me and encouraging me to finish my book. You guys are awesome!

To **Terrence Sani**, thank you for being a fantastic coach and mentor. You have inspired me to write this book and share my story. Thank you for motivating me to stop waiting for things to happen, and to make them happen. Thank you for your support and inspiration.

**Cesar Berrio**, gracias por hacer un gran ejemplo y maestro. Me has motivado a escribir este libro y siempre alcanzar mis metas. Gracias por la inspiracion.

To **Adam Sandler**, thank you for your inspiration and outlook on life. You've motivated me always to have a sense of humor and to continue pushing myself to new heights.

To **Cynthia Asante**, your book, *Exchange Setbacks for Winning*, has motivated me to finish writing my book. Thank you for being a wonderful inspiration and a great friend.

To **Cathy Niezen**, thank you for being an inspiration. You have motivated me to write my book and reach as many lives as possible. Thank you for being a great friend and mentor.

To **Don Lainer**, thank you for being a great coach and mentor. Thank you for your honesty and motivation to write my book. You have inspired me to follow my heart and dream big.

To **Ruth J. Verbree** and **Robert Verbree**, thank you for your support and motivation. You have inspired me to finish writing my book and share my story that will help millions. Thank you for your encouragement and inspiration.

To **Leo** and **Rebecca**, thank you for always having a great attitude and being a great example of having fun every morning and making the best of your day. You two are great inspirations.

To **Abraham Torres,** thank you for always believing in me and encouraging me to hang in there when things got tough. Thank you for your support, and for treating me like your own son. You are an amazing human being. I appreciate everything you've done for my family and me.

To **Robert Muncaster**, thank you for giving me the idea of organizing the title of the book, where it would also read, **U C Success**. Thanks for your advice and friendship.

# NEW BOOK
## Coming in 2020

www.ingramcontent.com/pod-product-compliance
Lightning Source LLC
Chambersburg PA
CBHW070756100426
42742CB00012B/2159